"YOU CANNOT LIVE A PERFECT DAY
WITHOUT DOING SOMETHING FOR SOMEONE
WHO WILL NEVER BE ABLE TO REPAY YOU."
—the words of John Wooden

Voted Coach of the Year six times by Associated Press. Awarded Sportsman of the Year by Sports Illustrated. Molder of such extraordinary players as Kareem Jabbar (Lew Alcindor), Gail Goodrich, Walt Hazzard and many others. Guiding force behind the longest winning streak in basketball history!

His dynamic story and his uplifting ideals for all men and athletes alike come to vivid life in

THEY CALL ME COACH

THEY CALL ME COACH

JOHN WOODEN

as told to Jack Tobin

A NATIONAL GENERAL COMPANY

*This low-priced Bantam Book
has been completely reset in a type face
designed for easy reading, and was printed
from new plates. It contains the complete
text of the original hard-cover edition.*
NOT ONE WORD HAS BEEN OMITTED.

RLI: VLM 7 (VLR 6–8)
IL 7–adult

THEY CALL ME COACH

*A Bantam Book / published by arrangement with
Word Books*

PRINTING HISTORY

Word edition published December 1972
2nd printing ...... January 1973
3rd printing .... April 1973
Bantam edition published October 1973

Grateful acknowledgment is made for permission to reprint the following copyrighted material:

"How to Be a Champion" and "The Great Competitor" by Grantland Rice, reprinted by permission of A. S. Barnes & Co., Inc., Cranbury, New Jersey; "They Ask Me Why I Teach" by Glennice L. Harmon, NEA JOURNAL, September 1948, reprinted by permission of NEA Journal, Washington, D. C.

Photographs courtesy ASUCLA Photographic Department, staff photographers Stan Troutman and Norm Schindler.

All rights reserved.
Copyright © 1972, 1973 by Word, Incorporated.
*This book may not be reproduced in whole or in part, by
mimeograph or any other means, without permission.
For information address: Word, Inc.
4800 W. Waco Drive, Waco, Texas 76703*

Published simultaneously in the United States and Canada

Bantam Books are published by Bantam Books, Inc., a National General company. Its trade-mark, consisting of the words "Bantam Books" and the portrayal of a bantam, is registered in the United States Patent Office and in other countries. Marca Registrada. Bantam Books, Inc., 666 Fifth Avenue, New York, N.Y. 10019.

PRINTED IN THE UNITED STATES OF AMERICA

This book is gratefully dedicated
to my wife, Nellie. Her love, faith and loyalty
through the years are primarily responsible
for what I am—be that good or be it bad.

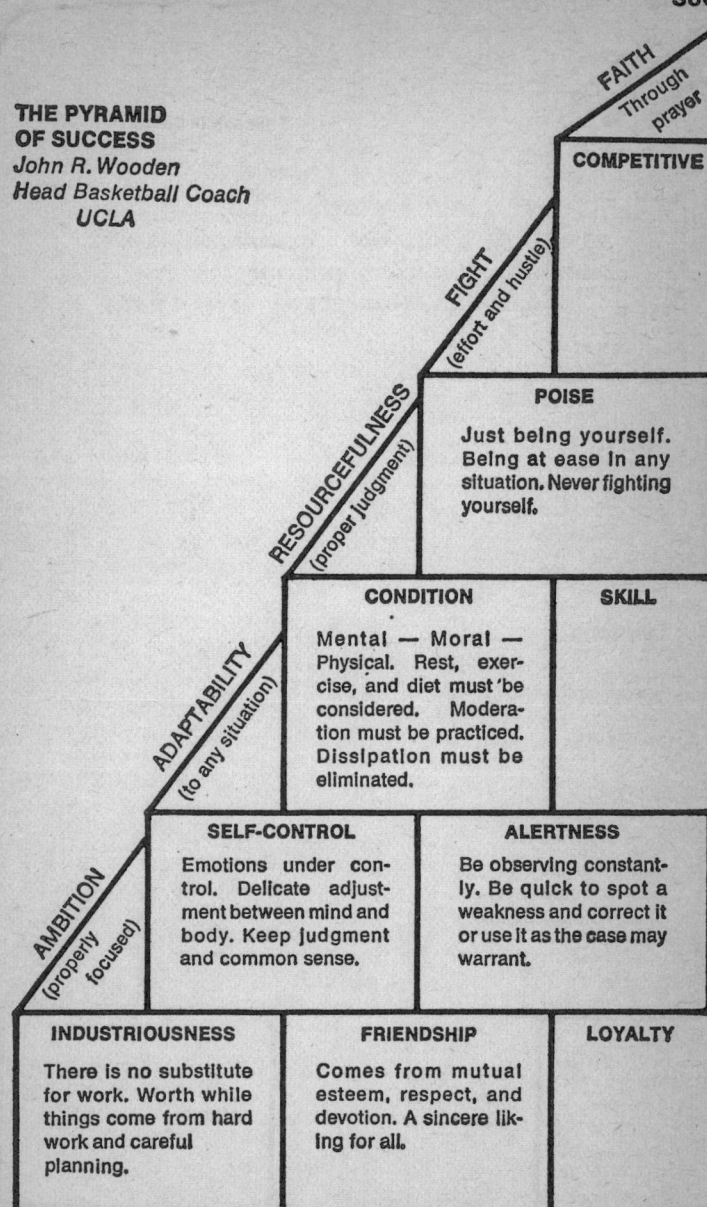

CESS

PATIENCE
Good things take time

GREATNESS
"When the going gets tough, the tough get going." Be at your best when your best is needed. Real love of a hard battle.

RELIABILITY
(others depend upon you)

CONFIDENCE
Respect without fear. Confident not cocky. May come from faith in yourself in knowing that you are prepared.

INTEGRITY
(speaks for itself)

TEAM SPIRIT
An eagerness to sacrifice personal interests or glory for the welfare of all. "The team comes first."

A knowledge of and the ability to properly execute the fundamentals. Be prepared. Cover every detail.

HONESTY
(in all ways)

INITIATIVE
Cultivate the ability to make decisions and think alone. Desire to excel.

INTENTNESS
Ability to resist temptation and stay with your course. Concentrate on your objective and be determined to reach your goal.

SINCERITY
(makes friends)

To yourself and to all those dependent upon you. Keep your self-respect.

COOPERATION
With all levels of your co-workers. Help others and see the other side.

ENTHUSIASM
Your heart must be in your work. Stimulate others.

Success is peace of mind which is a direct result of self-satisfaction in knowing you did your best to become the best that you are capable of becoming.

PREFACE

LIFE IS A UNITED EFFORT of many. My life has been inspired from my youthful days in high school, through university and into my coaching career by one person—my wife, Nellie. Together we have survived many trials, many misunderstandings, many separations; together we have weathered the great depression of the '30s with few material possessions and shared in the innumerable joys and disappointments that cross every life. Whatever problems have arisen—and there have been many in the life of a teacher and coach—Nellie has been beside me, providing encouragement in time of adversity and humbly accepting the accolades that have come in recent years.

Of nearly equal comfort and contentment have been my children—Nan, my daughter, and Jim, my son—and their families, whose lives have become so tightly entwined with my career. They are as much a part of my team as the many gifted players who have made possible our success in the eyes of the world.

In any attempt to recite one's life, it is not a case of carefully recording every incident whether good or bad, but of attempting to touch on those that now appear to loom large on the wide screen of life. In so doing, many hundreds of people, places, and things have been put aside—each with great consternation because everyone and everything that has crossed my life in the years since my birth October 14, 1910, has played a vital role. Every player with whom I have been associated, whether as a teammate or an opponent, has left a mark of value in my life span. Again, no single volume can properly record all the hours in a man's life.

May I thank each and every one of you who have played for me over the years at Dayton High School, South Bend Central High School, Indiana State University, and UCLA for the great memories; for the association that has been so beneficial to my memories; for the great effort you expended in pursuit of success on the basketball court; for the love and happiness each of you has showered on me by your tremendous personal effort.

To all who have assisted me in the coaching, care, and consideration of all my teams—secretaries, assistant and fellow coaches, trainers, managers, athletic directors, personal friends, and all the fans over all the years—my thanks.

No doubt all who have crossed my path in these years will recall or remember some event or episode and wonder why it was not included. There are hundreds that I recall and have set aside, for one reason or another. Some of the deletions resulted from advice given me by my late father, to whom I owe so much. "If you can't say something good about a man," he repeatedly told me, "it is best to say nothing."

Life is not all good nor is it all bad. What mortal man can separate the many gray areas into good and bad?

Hopefully, in these pages you will get some insight into the wonderful people who have walked with me. Hopefully, things will come to life that will enable you to participate in the way young America makes our way of life so marvelous.

May I just add one other thought:

> "O Lord, if I seem to lose my faith in Thee.
> do not Thou lose Thy faith in me."

December 1972   JOHN WOODEN

1

*Who can ask more of a man
than giving all within his span?
Giving all, it seems to me,
is not so far from victory.**

As I TURNED away from the post-game press conference and headed down that long corridor in Kansas City toward the dressing room, my feet and spirits dragged. For while I looked forward to congratulating the team on their victory, my thoughts were also on Fred Slaughter. What was he feeling at this moment?

Throughout the entire season, Fred had started every game. He had a brilliant year. Fred was a totally unselfish player with great team devotion and was frequently asked to do things for which a player receives little public attention. Even though he was short for a college center, barely 6 feet 5 inches tall, Fred was the blocker, screener, and rebounder—things seldom seen and appreciated by the crowd. But in this final game for the championship with Duke he had gotten off to a bad start. As the game moved along, it got worse instead of better. Finally, a change had to be made, so I pulled Fred and put in Doug McIntosh. And Doug did such a fine job that I left him in until the game was ours.

While I walked along toward the dressing room, George Moriarty's words were ringing in my mind, "Who can ask more of a man than giving all within his span? Giving all, it seems to me, is not so far from vic-

---

*George Moriarty, "The Road Ahead of the Road Behind."

tory." And yet I knew that Fred was not alone in his disappointment. Having grown up not too far away in Topeka, Kansas, where he had attended high school, he was well aware that the crowd had been pretty well sprinkled with Slaughter relatives and fans.

Pushing open the dressing room door, I ran right into Fred. He had evidently been waiting for me. "Coach," he said, "before someone gets the wrong impression, I want you to know that I understand. You had to leave Doug in there because he played so well, and I didn't. I wanted to play in the worst way, but I do understand, and if anyone says I was upset, it's not true. Disappointed, yes, but upset, no. And I was very happy for Doug."

You know, there are a lot of peaks and valleys in every coach's life. But this was *the* peak—the ultimate. We had won our first, and my first, NCAA title by whipping Duke 98 to 83 and closed out the 1964 season with a perfect 30 and 0 record. But my concern for Fred had damaged all of that until this moment. Now I felt really great!

You get very close to the boys who play for you. Despite all efforts to the contrary a coach becomes attached to them—at times, thinking about a player as if he were his own son. And you become very concerned about their feelings and disappointments. Fred Slaughter and the other boys on that 1964 team made me feel that way. They had done everything I asked of them. And they had done it my way in spite of the fact that at times they may have questioned it. As a team, they were impressive, but never more so than in coming from behind late in the game to beat Kansas State 90 to 84 in the semifinals and recovering from a poor start to overwhelm Duke for the championship.

Interestingly, back in January of 1963 I had predicted that the 1964 team could be champions. Each year I write a little message to myself on how I expect the team to do before the basketball season begins and seal it in an envelope. On this occasion, however, I added something extra. Pete Blackman, who had played forward on our team before going in the service, was stationed in Hawaii. In reply to a poetic letter he had written me, I sent him a free verse letter dated January 17, 1963. The last stanza predicted what could happen.

Dear Pete—

This legal pad, my friend, must do,
To convey my remarks to you,
For I shall speak of many things,
Of players who would all be kings,
Of boys who work and boys who don't,
Of boys who will and boys who won't,
Of many things, I'm sure that you
May wonder at, but know are true.

At Washington we lost a pair,
We were quite cold, as was the air,
Not one could hit and Fred was flat,
And played more like "Sir Fred of Fat."
Too many boys just want to start,
If not, they don't want any part,
And then at times some have a flair,
That makes one wonder if they care.

One forward seems to think that he
Surpasses all at comedy,
Another does not like to run,
But is involved in endless fun.
A mother thinks her son should start,
Or from the team he should depart,
From these remarks it's plain to see
It's more than simple rivalry.

One boy has drawn some other's ire,
Because he never seems to tire.
He gives his best throughout the day,
He only knows that way to play;
A starting spot some others seek,

By partial effort through the week,
They wonder why my eyes shoot fire,
When they question drills that I require.

Sir Mil of Wee now feels that he
A starter evermore should be,
But young soph Gail of fingers long,
Cannot agree, he knows that's wrong;
Some care not if we win or lose,
Their interest is in whom I use,
When the ball is tossed by the referee,
A starter's spot is all they see.

Our problems still remain the same,
A fact you've heard me oft proclaim,
We first must think just of the team,
And sacrifice the selfish dream;
But know that if the team does well,
In every way each must excel,
It matters not who is to blame,
Each one must truly play the game.

Now is the time when some show nerve,
To hope their profs won't use the curve;
Final exams began this week,
The grades of some we soon must seek,
And I will feel a bit of shame,
When some boys will professors blame,
And feel, of course, the profs should swerve,
And give them not what they deserve.

Sir Fred just called to say that he
And Gail at practice could not be;
In the morn at eight they have an exam,
For which today they wish to cram,
They know for this I can't say "no,"
And I'd be wrong if I did so;
Miss practice—for study! I'll always agree,
But they've had no exams in the past days—three!!

It was expected and it came,
Jack's knee is sore, in fact he's lame,
He cannot practice on this day,
But is sure this weekend he can play,
He called along with Chuck and Keith,
From practice they all seek relief,
No—that remark I should not claim,
They really like to play the game.

However, Pete, there's optimism
Beneath my valid criticism,
I want to say—yes, I'll foretell,
Eventually this team will jell,
And when they do, they will be great,
A championship could be their fate,
With every starter coming back,
Yes, Walt and Gail and Keith and Jack
And Fred and Freddie and some more,
We could be champs in sixty-four.

Actually, each team I have ever coached has had its own particular character. But while I have never said that any one of them was better than another, I guess I'll have to admit to having a special feeling for my first NCAA champions. It was a team of tremendous courage and poise that met every challenge. While it was a short team, they played tall in style and determination and were never rattled when we were behind. There was never a show of panic or any inclination to abandon the game plan. In fact there were times when I may have teetered on the verge of a change of tactic, but they held steady and were confident. Above all, each player believed firmly in our pressing defense. They were confident that it would produce the results we wanted.

Some fans and sports writers have said that I used the press for the first time with the 1964 team, but this wasn't the case. Years before I had used it with my high school teams, and in 1963 it was introduced as the basic defense with our UCLA squad. And toward the end of that season it really began to pay off.

In short, their defense was aggressive, and they were a fine passing team with tremendous hustle, drive, and determination. I'm certain that thought of defeat never entered their minds.

Each of the five starters and two backup men were strong willed and strong minded athletes. They were individuals who melded together on the basketball court with superb precision.

WALT HAZZARD Walt, a senior in 1964, was a fine team leader and an outstanding passer. But most important, he thoroughly understood what I wanted to accomplish. He was my kind of a guard.

Philadelphia had been home for Walt; his father was a minister there. And through a rather complex and at times confusing set of circumstances, he ended up at UCLA as a sophomore.

Willie Naulls, the first of my players to make it in the National Basketball Association, was playing with the New York Knickerbockers at the time. He and his cousin, Woody Sauldsberry of the Philadelphia Warriors, were impressed with Walt's ability as a high school player. It was worked out for Walt to come west, but, unfortunately, his grades were substandard as far as the high requirements at UCLA were concerned, so he enrolled for a year at Santa Monica City College. Being from out of state, he was ineligible to play at Santa Monica so we arranged for him to play that season with the old Kirby's Shoe team in the local AAU league.

Up to that time I hadn't seen Walt in action, but it only took one game to convince me that he had it. "Walter," I told him after that first game, "you don't have to worry about making the team when you get to UCLA next season. And, you've got a scholarship all the way." I felt certain that other coaches would soon be after him, and I wanted to reassure him of my interest.

So, with no freshman experience and no familiarity with our system, he became the starting guard and floor leader on my 1961–62 team and did a fine job after we got off to a slow start.

The next year, however, Walt reverted to his one bad habit. When he came to us he had a tendency toward fancy play and did a lot of behind-the-back and blind passing and fancy dribbling. He had found out during his sophomore year that I did not permit this type of play, but somehow, perhaps because of his success as a sophomore, he began to revert to his old habits.

Our first road trip game that year was with the University of Colorado at Boulder. Walter got carried away and was too fancy for me so I pulled him out, and he sat the rest of the game out on the bench. We lost and it was tough to take because our chances of winning had been greatly diminished with him on the bench. They beat us rather handily, however, and his presence might not have made any difference.

The next night we played at Colorado State. Again I had Walt on the bench at the start and for much of the game. We lost this one too, by one point in a double overtime.

Shortly after, I had a call from Rev. Walter R. Hazzard in Philadelphia. It seems that Walt had called him and said he was going to quit because I wouldn't let him play basketball the way he knew best. But Mr. Hazzard said, "I'm on your side, Coach Wooden. I told Walter not to come home if he quits—there would be no place for him here." Of course, he did not mean it that strong, but he wanted his son to stand up to adversity.

Walter stayed on and had three great years.

FRED SLAUGHTER While lacking in height as a center, Fred had other attributes which made him the hub around which we all revolved. He was quick and did a marvelous job of setting up the others and of rebounding. As a former high school track man, he had a keen sense of anticipation. But above all, he, like the others, was innately very intelligent.

Slaughter came to us from Topeka, Kansas, although his mother lived in Los Angeles where Fred had gone through grade school. Our scouting reports indicated that he was probably even a better track man, with decathlon potential, than a basketball player. So he came to us on a half basketball, half track scholarship. If he had made good in only one sport, that sport would take over his scholarship grant. He was not a spectacular player, but was a fine team player, and, after overcoming a problem or two, accepted his role and filled it admirably.

KEITH ERICKSON   At forward, Keith was a fiery, fearless player, and the tougher the opponent, the better he played. Keith led our defense both by example and voice. As the safety man in our pressing defense, he was the only man with a full view of the floor and was in command of what was developing.

At times Erickson's fiery personality became really inflamed. And when Keith was upset because he wasn't given the opportunity to score or felt he was not being properly appreciated by the others, he let everyone in sight know exactly how he felt.

We took Erickson when no one else wanted him and put him on a basketball scholarship for a year with baseball to take over if he did not measure up in basketball. One of my early UCLA boys, George Stanich, coached Keith at El Camino Junior College, but he didn't recommend him highly. Although George felt that Keith was a fine athlete and might even become great if he could get his emotions under control, he had some reservations about his ability to do that.

In looking back on it I guess I was challenged with the idea of trying to control and direct that spirit. And I became convinced that I could work with him and help him develop into a truly great player. I was always fond of this highly spirited young man and became very proud of him both on and off the court. He played the game at both ends of the floor in a highly competitive way.

JACK HIRSCH Probably the best way to describe Jack is to share an early confrontation we had. The team was at training table one night having dinner. Jack didn't like the menu, so he pushed his plate back and said, "I'm not going to eat this slop."

I didn't like that and promptly told him so. "You're right, Jack. You are not going to eat it. Get out, and if you still feel that way about it, just don't come back to training table."

"I can eat better than this at home," he told me.

"I know you can, Jack. You can have steak every night if you want it. You can also drive a Grand Prix while the rest of us drive some little car. We understand that, but you don't eat here any more until your attitude changes."

He said he didn't care and stalked out. I guess he was off training table for a couple of weeks. Then one day there was a knock on my office door. The door was open, and when I looked up, I saw it was Hirsch. It was out of character for Jack to knock; usually he just barged right in.

"Coach, I'm sorry."

"Sorry about what, Jack?"

"What do you want me to do, coach? Get down on my knees and beg? You know what I'm sorry about."

At that moment I came to know the real Jack Hirsch. Not too many people liked him at that time, and when I told him so, he said he just didn't care.

Actually, Jack lacked confidence at that time and tried to bull his way with roughness. In my opinion he was so afraid of not being accepted that he made sure people had a reason not to like him.

Hirsch came to us after two years at Valley Junior College. The coach from San Fernando Valley State had talked with him, but the only scholarship offer he had was from UCLA. Although he was short for a forward, only 6 feet 3 inches, he played a great deal bigger because of his jumping skill, his long arms, and fine timing. One of our unsung heroes—Jack wasn't spectacular, but he was a great team man who played the game every inch from end line to end line. Although he seemed to lack seriousness at times, he had it when it was needed and, like Keith, often made the big play for us.

I've had a lot of favorites over the years, and Jack is one of them. I'm still very fond of him.

GAIL GOODRICH Goodrich teamed with Walt Hazzard at guard. He was inherently a very confident player, wanting the ball and resenting it if he thought Walt was monopolizing it. Gail felt certain that he could do more with the ball, but he finally came to realize that if he worked hard and got into the open, Hazzard would see to it that he got it. This made Goodrich, in my opinion, a much better basketball player, and I believe it has been borne out by his play in the pros. Of course, his intense competitive spirit and determination were necessary as well.

Of all the boys who made up that first championship team, Gail Goodrich's background is the most unique. It was during his junior year in high school at the Los Angeles City championships that Gail first attracted my attention. I was sitting in the Sports Arena with Paul Neal, a friend from my church. We had come to watch a couple of other boys whose names I've now forgotten. Pointing toward the floor, I said, "That little guy with Poly is the smartest player on the floor. He's only a junior. I haven't heard much about him, but I'm going to watch him another year. If he grows a little and shows normal improvement, he may be the best prospect out there."

A few minutes later a man sitting behind us tapped me on the shoulder. "Coach Wooden, you don't know us, but did you really mean what you said about that small guard out there?"

"Yes, I do."

"Well, we're his parents."

The next week Mr. or Mrs. Goodrich called and

asked if they could bring Gail over with his transcripts, Jerry Norman, my assistant, and I went over them carefully and discovered that Gail would be a mid-year graduate the following school year. And unlike most other school systems, the basketball season in Los Angeles would be completed by the time of his graduation.

Gail's final high school season was tremendous. He was the star of the city tournament, and by this time everybody wanted to talk to him. Bobby Kolf, Forrest Twogood's assistant at the University of Southern California, worked hard to persuade Gail to go to USC where his father had been a basketball star and captain of the team. But that chance remark of mine the year before and our continued interest throughout his final semester paid off. Gail enrolled in UCLA in February.

KENNY WASHINGTON It was during the summer of 1963 that Walt Hazzard called from Philadelphia and told me about Washington. "He's from Booker T. Washington High in Beaufort, South Carolina. He's 6 feet 5 inches tall, a greater shooter than Gary Cunningham (one of my former players and now my assistant), as good a ball handler as I am, and weighs about one ninety to two hundred." It seems that Walt had met Kenny when he was visiting friends in Philadelphia and was impressed by him.

After checking we learned that Washington had the grades so we admitted him on a one year "make good" scholarship. He came west on a Greyhound bus. Jerry Norman met him at the station, and he looked scared to death. Evidently he had ridden all the way from Beaufort in the back end of the bus. I guess he figured he couldn't sit anywhere else. Instead of being 6 feet 5 inches and 200, he was 6 feet 3 inches, weighed about 160, and was extremely shy. Apparently, Walt had wanted to make certain that we would be impressed.

One day at freshman practice I saw Kenny standing over to one side with tears streaming down his cheeks. "What's the matter, Kenny?" I asked.

"It's going to be 160 days until I get back to Beaufort."

"No, Kenny, it's not," I responded. "I don't know how long it took you to get out here, but it will take you just that long to get back. If you don't shape up, you can ship out tomorrow on the first Greyhound."

I'm convinced that this remark helped him grow up a little and get his feet on the ground. He and I have laughed about that many times since. Actually, he's another great favorite of mine because of the way he developed and became one of the great "sixth men" in basketball.

DOUG McINTOSH Although the "seventh man" on our 1964 team, Doug's big moment came when he stepped in for Fred Slaughter in the championship game with Duke and played so well for most of the rest of the game.

Dough came to us from Lily, Kentucky, on a "make good" scholarship. His freshman year wasn't the least bit impressive, and we debated about extending the scholarship. Believe me, I'm happy it all worked out, and he stayed on.

In all, this was a remarkable group of men. Erickson, Hazzard, and Goodrich went on to successful careers in professional basketball. Fred Slaughter graduated from Columbia Law School and is now an assistant dean in the UCLA Law School. Jack Hirsch is a very successful business man. Presently, Kenny Washington is in law school at Loyola in Los Angeles, and Doug McIntosh went to theological school and is now teaching in a seminary.

Sometimes I wonder if the good Lord isn't almost as much the coach as I am. He certainly has smiled on me and truly moves in mysterious ways His wonders to perform.

2

A careful man I want to be,
A little fellow follows me;
I do not dare to go astray,
For fear he'll go the self-same way.

ONCE AGAIN I was faced with an agonizing decision. It was 1965—just one year after that first championship—and we were now fighting it out in the Portland Coliseum with Michigan. The NCAA championship would be ours again if we won this game.

Doug McIntosh, whose spectacular substitution for Slaughter in the 1964 championship game contributed so much to that win, was our regular starting center. He'd had a good year, but he didn't get off to a good start in this decisive Michigan game. And just as with Slaughter the year before, I had to pull Doug and substitute Mike Lynn, a sophomore. Mike did well, and I played him almost all the rest of the game.

And so, as I headed toward the dressing room, my feelings matched those of 1964. But, like Fred, Doug understood and told me that I had no choice. There wasn't even a hint of resentment, and Doug was happy that the team had done so well.

These two incidents, along with many others that have occurred during my many years as a teacher and coach, have caused me to realize just how great the so-called father-son relationship is between coach and his players. And this takes me back to the early and formative years of my own life.

My roots are deep in Indiana soil, for on October 14, 1910, I was born in a little place called Hall where my father worked as a tenant farmer for a man named Cash Ludlow. But a couple of years later my family moved three or four miles away to Monrovia, Indiana, where dad took a job as a rural mail carrier in addition to working a small farm. It is here that my earliest memories come into focus. One of them is dad's horse and buggy, and how I loved to go with him on his mail route. My love for a horse and buggy never ceased. I had but one dream, to own a buggy with red wheels and a little black mare to pull it. A cousin of mine had such a rig. Once in a while he would let me drive it to White Lick, a stream that was a tributary to the White River. I'd drive it out on a gravel bar and wash and shine it until it sparkled. Monrovia was just a small community, perhaps five hundred people in those days, and the people were all so friendly. Anyway, between the mail route and our small farm I thought we had a wonderful life.

About the time I was to begin my second year of grade school my mother inherited from her father a sixty-acre farm near Centerton, Indiana. Those were truly the rural farm days. We had no electricity, no inside plumbing, and we got our water from a hand pump. In addition to corn, wheat, and alfalfa, we grew watermelons and tomatoes.

Farming was a family affair. Even though I was pretty small, I was good at milking cows and cranking the milk separator. Actually, I came to love most everything we had to do on the farm with the possible exception of weeding and bugging potatoes and worming the tomatoes. Then, too, picking tomatoes was backbreaking work. I guess this is why I always have a great feeling of empathy for those stoop workers laboring out in the hot sun in the fields of the Central California San Joaquin Valley.

Dad believed in work, and he saw to it that my brothers—Maurice, or Cat as we called him most of the time, Daniel, and Billy—and I were kept busy. But as with all brothers we had our disagreements, although none of them were very serious. However, I do remember one incident that happened when I was in the sixth or seventh grade that has had a great bearing on my entire life. We were all in the barn cleaning out the horses' stalls, and Cat flipped a pitch fork of manure over and it hit me in the face.

I went right after him and called him an s.o.b. Dad heard me and immediately stopped the ruckus. After listening to both sides of the story, he gave me a good thrashing for what I said. My brother Cat got a whipping too, but I still think his wasn't as hard as mine.

Dad certainly didn't condone what Cat had done, but neither would he put up with my loss of control or swearing. I think this one incident—little though it may seem to be—taught me a lesson that has kept me from using profanity through the years.

Actually, my father has had a profound influence on my life. Both my philosophy of life and of coaching came largely from him. Even as a small boy I always had great respect for him because I knew he would always be fair with me and had my best interests at heart. And I soon learned that if he couldn't say something good about another person, he wouldn't say anything at all—a philosophy I've tried to follow.

A truly gentle man, dad read the Bible daily; he wanted us to read it, and we did. That is probably why I keep a copy on my desk today. It's not a decoration, but is well marked and read. The fact that I never heard dad swear, along with the incident in the barn, surely accounts for the fact that even today when I get mad, the strongest thing I can say is "goodness gracious sakes alive."

I remember so well what dad gave me for graduation from that little country grade school in Centerton. It was a piece of paper on which he had written a creed that he suggested I try to live by. It read:

1. Be true to yourself.
2. Make each day your masterpiece.
3. Help others.

4. Drink deeply from good books, especially the Bible.
5. Make friendship a fine art.
6. Build a shelter against a rainy day.
7. Pray for guidance, count and give thanks for your blessings every day.

I carried dad's handwritten original of that in my wallet for many years until it wore out. Then I had copies made, and I keep one in my wallet today along with another little quotation which further exemplifies my father's spirit.

> Four things a man must learn to do
> If he would make his life more true:
> To think without confusion more clearly,
> To love his fellow-man sincerely,
> To act from honest motives purely,
> To trust in God and heaven securely.

I wish I could say that I have always lived by that creed and quotation. I can't, but I have tried.

My dad did love his fellow-man sincerely. He was honest to the nth degree and had a great trust and faith in the Lord. And he taught us many lessons in integrity and honesty which we never forgot. Even though he was never able financially to help his sons through college, he is undoubtedly responsible for the fact that all of us graduated from college, got advanced degrees, and entered the teaching profession.

One such unforgettable lesson occurred while we were at Centerton. Parker's and Breedlove's were the two general stores in town. And whenever we could scrape together a nickel, we would ask Mr. Parker to mix up an assortment of candy. We'd get a handful each of licorice, jelly beans, peppermint and chocolate—probably as much as a dollar would buy today.

But, on this particular hot and humid Indiana day I'd walked into town to see my friend Freddy Gooch.

His parents had a charge account at Breedlove's, so when we went in there he charged a bottle of pop. I was thirsty and finally weakened, charging a bottle of cream soda on my parents' account. It was good, but I was scared to death as I walked home later because I knew my parents hadn't given me permission to buy the pop, and they really couldn't afford it.

Finally, after I had been home a while I confessed what I had done, expecting a real hard whipping. But dad and mother understood my being tempted, and they just explained firmly why my actions were wrong. Believe me, that made a big impression on me, and I never did that again.

While money was hard to come by in those days, we always ate well. All farmers did. We had a big garden, grew all our own vegetables, had a lot of fruit trees, grew all kinds of berries and, of course, if one farmer had peaches and another pears, they'd trade.

We had a big cellar where we'd store potatoes, pumpkins, things that would keep. Then we had a smokehouse where we'd smoke meat for the winter. Of course, mom spent hours and hours canning. All the boys had to help. We'd pick the fruit, help cut it up, and then seal the jars either with paraffin or those glass lids that were made by the Ball Company in Muncie, Indiana.

One of the jobs we boys had was picking wild berries. In those days in Indiana you could find all kinds of wild blackberries, raspberries, and strawberries. Mom would make jams or jellies and also can them whole so she could make them into cobblers. We had a lot of cobblers because we all were especially fond of them.

I still contend that while we couldn't go out and buy a lot of the things the way we do today, we ate well. And mom was a cook that was appreciated.

Dad always made sure we had some fun mixed with our work, so it was during these early days on the farm that my love for sports emerged. I was probably around eight years old when I first learned something about basketball. Dad made a basket for us out of an old tomato basket with the bottom knocked out and nailed it up on a wall at one end of the hay loft in the barn. Our basketball was made out of old rags stuffed inside a pair of mother's black cotton hose. She would sew it up, by hand, into as round a form as possible. It's hard to imagine now but I still think we were able to dribble that thing.

Then when I was in the third or fourth grade, dad got a forge, and one of the first things he did was make a ring out of iron for a basket. That iron ring was pretty close to regulation. It went up in the loft and we made sure we used hay from that end up first so we could play basketball.

Even in those early years my dreams were entwined with school, basketball, baseball and college. I don't think I really knew what going to college meant but Earl Warriner, our teacher, principal, and coach often talked about it, especially at basketball practice.

One of the essentials of every school day was what Mr. Warriner called the "morning sing." I was a terrible singer. So were the others on the basketball team, but we'd mouth the words. Finally, he had enough. One day, he stopped the sing and took us one at a time to the front of the class.

"Will you sing?" he asked me when my turn came.

"No." I was stubborn, so he laid it on me with a special willow switch he had cut for the job.

"Now will you sing?" he asked after a few cracks.

"I'll try." But just to make sure he hit me a couple more licks.

"Will you sing?"

"I'll sing."

I've never forgotten that. A year or so after that whipping, I got a card in the mail with a picture of an opera singer and it read, "You must remember this one thing, In opera you have to sing."

It was signed anonymously, but I always believed Mr. Warriner sent it but never could prove it.

One of our favorite times in grade school was Halloween. We pulled all the usual tricks. One of the best, however, was what we called "ticktacking." That's where you grooved an empty spool of thread, put it on someone's door and spun it by pulling the string from thirty or forty feet away. It made an awful racket. There was one person in town who seemed to be quite a crank, so naturally one year we decided to ticktack him. I drew the short straw and had to creep up on the porch to place it on the door. Just as I did he came around the corner, shotgun in hand.

"What are you doing?" he yelled.

I took off, leaped his three-foot-high fence, and just as I hit the ground he blasted the shotgun, and I was hit in the back with a barrage of pellets. I ran for a block or two before diving into a bush to hide. Carefully I felt my backside for blood but couldn't find any.

A little later when I sneaked back to where the gang was hanging out, I found the imagined crank and the rest of the boys really laughing it up. I'd been duped, and they were all in on it. The pellets I felt when the gun went off were pebbles the gang had thrown. It was quite a while before I would forgive my friends or even play ball with them. But that didn't last long because basketball and baseball came close to being my first loves.

But during those early days baseball was really my favorite. All of the boys loved it so dad leveled off one end of a field and made a baseball diamond for us. Our ball was usually a makeshift affair, although occasionally we could save up and get a real one. And our bats were whittled out of a tree limb that had a nice, straight grain. It would take all winter to whittle a good bat with knife, file and a plane. Our field was pretty crude and we didn't have a backstop. Some of our games were almost funny, but we loved it and learned to play well.

By the time I was thirteen or fourteen I was good enough to play on the Centerton town team even though several of the players were in their twenties. I always played shortstop, and that ball really used to come humming at me off of those homemade bats. But I always dug in and went after it. I knew if I didn't, somebody other than John Wooden would be in that lineup. There was a lot of competition, but I hung in there, became a farm boy sportsman, and dreamed big dreams about the future. My older brother Cat was always a great help to me as were my mother and dad. Cat helped me from a technical point of view, while mother and dad furnished great patience and understanding.

3

*Worm or beetle—drought or tempest
—on a farmer's land may fall,
Each is loaded full o' ruin,
but a mortgage beats 'em all.**

MY DAD WAS born to be a farmer. He seemed to have a way with both land and animals, which can probably best be explained by telling about our two teams of mules—Jack and Kate and Betz and Hanna. Kate was a balky animal, especially with children. When we boys worked the fields with them, Kate would balk and lie down. Dad might be a half mile away, but all he had to do was just start walking across the field and Kate would get right up. She would never lie down for him, but she sure gave us a bad time.

I don't know how he did it, but I do know that he never resorted to force with any animal. There was a gentle way about him that they seemed to understand.

Farming came to an end for dad and us in 1924. There was a depression, probably not as severe as the one later in the thirties, but we sure thought it was bad.

There was a mortgage on the farm and things weren't going well, so dad decided to raise hogs. He borrowed the money, bought the feed and vaccine for the cholera shots which all hogs must have. But instead of protecting them, the vaccine gave them cholera and they all died.

Since another investment had turned out to be with a fraudulent company, dad couldn't repay the loan so we

---
* Will Carleton, "The Tramp's Story."

lost the farm and moved into Martinsville. I had started to Martinsville High the year before as a freshman and had been commuting on the interurban. It was eight miles from the Centerton stop to the terminal in Martinsville and we'd catch it out in front of Breedlove's general store.

Martinsville was the county seat and had a population then of about 5,000. There was a town square with the courthouse in center. Everything revolved around that square. There were hitching racks and watering troughs on each corner. A few of the people had cars then, and they'd drive in early every Saturday evening and try to be first to get the prime parking place in front of Riley's Cafe or Shireman's Ice Cream Parlor.

The Blackstone, our favorite pool hall, was next to Shireman's, and just on down the north side of the square was Riley's Cafe where once in a great while dad would take us all to dinner. Little did I realize then what an expense one of those dinners was to mom and dad. I knew we weren't wealthy, but I wasn't fully aware at that age of just how hard pressed we were for the money to take care of the normal day-to-day essentials.

Dad got a job at Homelawn Sanitarium where he worked in the bath house and gave massages. Because there were artesian wells in Martinsville, it had become a resort where a lot of people from Chicago, Indianapolis, Detroit, Cleveland, and other midwestern cities came for baths. Evidently the baths were helpful to people who had arthritis and rheumatism. I guess you could compare Martinsville to Hot Springs, Arkansas, or White Sulphur Springs, West Virginia, but I doubt if it was as plush.

Dad was real good at his job at Homelawn. He always had compassion for others, especially those who were infirm. There were people who came to Homelawn and my dad for all the years he worked there, and that was more than 25 years.

While dad received a salary—and I have no idea

what it was now—a good deal of our income was based on the tips he'd receive each day. We always had one of those large calendars on the kitchen wall where mom would keep track of the tips. We'd be able to compare them to a year, two years, or even three years before. There were a few people who might give dad a five-dollar tip, and if one of these didn't come back the next year or the next time they were expected, we'd know it from the calendar.

While we never returned to the farm—dad worked at the sanitarium until he died in 1950—we often had a garden and grew many of our vegetables. And mom still canned the fruit and made jellies and jam. Actually, we never got the farm life out of our systems, except we never missed doing the chores. While we hadn't objected to them as kids, we much preferred life in Martinsville where baseball and basketball came next to study, at least a part of the time.

Martinsville has a very special place for another very important reason, however. It was there at a carnival the summer of my freshman year in high school that I met the girl I was to marry. Nellie Riley was a pert, vivacious, captivating girl with a very vibrant personality.

By contrast, I was terribly shy—painfully so, in fact. I recall vividly one summer day when I was out plowing on the farm in Centerton, and Nellie and some other kids who lived in Martinsville drove out in a car to see me. They parked on the knoll where they could see me, but I just kept right on plowing. Nellie thought I had no time for her. Little did she know that much as I wanted to stop and talk with her, I was just too bashful.

When I look back on those early days, I know just how fortunate I am that Nellie Riley was a patient and determined young lady. It wasn't that I was so hard to catch, but I was very ill at ease with girls.

Even after we became better acquainted and were going together, we had a problem. Nellie's house backed right up to where Glenn Curtis lived. Curtis, the basketball coach at Martinsville High, had a rule that you couldn't date during basketball season and you had to be home by 8:00 P.M.

In a little town like Martinsville it was pretty hard to do anything which the whole town didn't know about. From my sophomore year on there was no doubt in Nellie's mind or mine that we were in love, and I always felt that Curtis would peek in the window of the Riley house to see if I was there. And I was there pretty often.

It had to be pretty tough on a popular girl like Nellie not to go out on dates during basketball season—a rather long time, in those days. Our season began right after school started and lasted until the end of February or early March.

Now while Nellie enjoyed basketball, she also liked to dance, go to the movies and just have fun. But dancing was something I never really liked, although I enjoyed watching other people dance. I felt like I had two left feet and never could keep time with the music. Nellie had trouble believing that, especially after watching me run some of the intricate play patterns Curtis designed and never botch them up.

So between the no dates and the no dancing, we'd have spats from time to time, and Nellie would have dates with other people. We always managed to make up, of course. I think I had a date a time or two during one of our spats but Nellie was the only girl I ever really went with.

One little intimacy that we maintain to this day began in the first game I ever played at Martinsville High. Wanting to get Nellie's attention before the center jump that first game, I looked over at the band where she was playing the cornet, and winked at her. She took her thumb and index finger to form an "O"— meaning good luck, everything is okay. I waved back. Now I just wave my rolled-up program.

Hundreds and maybe thousands of fans today must wonder what in the world John Wooden is doing making that little sign just before a UCLA basketball team takes the floor. Sometimes—at the Houston Astrodome, for instance—we've had to do a bit of searching. In fact, in the NCAA championships there in 1971, Nellie had to stand up and wave her arms like a Navy signalman before I could see her.

Nellie's inspiration and push—more than anything else—have contributed to what success I've enjoyed in life. She never let me get discouraged, even during the darkest hour. Many times during my college days at Purdue when I wanted to quit, she kept my spirits up, encouraging me to stay and work for my degree, even though most of the time it was by telephone from Martinsville to West Lafayette.

Coach Curtis had been fearful we would get married after I graduated from high school. I remember his going to Nellie's mother and talking to her about the situation. He explained that while I might earn eighteen or twenty dollars a week, I would make far more later on if I went to college and got my degree. We have often laughed about this because at that time Mrs. Riley felt she would be marvelously happy if I could ever earn that much.

Our families, like many families in Martinsville, were quite close. We belonged to the same church, attended the same socials, visited the same friends and of course shopped in the same stores. While Martinsville was a little place and you could walk almost anywhere in the town in five or ten minutes, both of our families had telephones and I'm sure our parents wondered how we could talk so long on the phone when we had just separated a few minutes before.

There was a little park in Martinsville where they held band concerts on Saturday nights and we'd often go there. Once in a while we'd just take a walk out in the country or a lot of us would get together, pack lunches and go out on a hayride on a team and wagon that belonged to someone in high school who still lived on a farm. And there were tennis courts at the high school where we'd play occasionally. I wasn't much of a tennis player and Nellie never had much trouble beating me. Whether I won or lost playing Nellie didn't much concern me because just being with her was the important thing.

4

*Stubborness we deprecate,
Firmness we condone.
The former is our neighbor's trait,
The latter is our own.*

MARTINSVILLE, like so many small Indiana communities, lived, breathed, and died basketball. The gymnasium could hold more people than there were residents in the city. This was true in many Indiana towns, even back in those days, because the surrounding populace were avid fans.

One year the sectional tournament was held in Martinsville. Paragon, a little place two or three miles south of Martinsville, was in the first round early Saturday morning. During the game, the Paragon bank was robbed. It was claimed the robbers were successful because all the people were at the game in Martinsville, even the police.

Robbing banks was a common occurrence in Indiana in those days. John Dillinger, probably the most notorious bank robber of the time, was from Mooresville, which was about seven miles north of Centerton. Dillinger received his first jail sentence, as I recall, from Judge Williams in Martinsville. One of the judge's sons was in school with me and later became an admiral in the U.S. Navy. I remember after the judge had imposed sentence that Dillinger threatened to kill him when he got out of jail.

While basketball was vital to life in Martinsville, there were a few other things such as weekly band concerts, carnivals, Saturday gatherings, family reunions, square and round dances, county fairs and so on that provided a bit of spice.

For years, Martinsville had done very well in Indiana basketball, primarily because of a fine coach, Glenn Curtis. He had a great deal of influence in my coaching career at Indiana State and UCLA. In fact, I succeeded Curtis as coach at Indiana State. That was rather ironic because at one point my basketball career almost ended because of him.

Actually, in my sophomore season it did end—for two weeks. I didn't like Glenn Curtis then as a person, but I respected his basketball ability. My dislike stemmed from problems my older brother, Cat, had with Curtis. Curtis always used him as the sixth man. Cat was a fine player and often came in as the sixth man to win many games. He went on to Franklin College in Indiana where he did very well, but he was always a sixth man with Curtis.

I felt then, and I still do, that Curtis never gave Cat the opportunity he merited based on his ability in comparison with the other players. I learned long ago that the best players don't necessarily make the best team, and I believe Cat would have made Martinsville a better team.

Early in my sophomore year another player, who was considered a Curtis pet, and I tangled. I didn't lack in courage in those days. This fellow might be able to whip me, but he didn't scare me. Curtis took his side. I knew he was wrong, and the rest of the squad knew it, but Curtis was firm.

"Well," I said, "you're not going to get the chance to give me the treatment you gave my brother." With that I stalked off the floor—there would be no more basketball for me. I stayed away for two weeks. Curtis talked to me several times. Even though I was very upset, he was persistent, and I finally agreed to come back.

I was stubborn and stood up for what I felt was right. I'm sure this incident accounts for the fact that throughout my coaching career I have tried to understand the young men who have stood up to me. That's why I listen to their side, and why I've almost always taken back a boy who has walked off the team.

While we look upon college players today as young men because of their size, they are really still boys in maturity. You have to bend. They have to bend. When both bend within proper bounds, you become a solid unit.

Curtis's greatest strength was in handling the young, immature players—the obstinate ones like me. I never doubted Curtis's coaching ability, even when I stalked out. He was an excellent teacher; later he became principal and superintendent of schools in Martinsville before moving to Indiana State. After a short career as a pro coach, he returned to Martinsville in the same positions.

One of his coaching concepts I never could accept was trying to fire a team up emotionally for a game. I never believed in it, and I still don't. But Curtis could make you tingle before an important game.

However, we did have one great common bond. He often quoted poetry at practice to illustrate a point. I have always been a lover of poetry, and I believe this influenced me to accept him and his ideas. He was a solid teacher of fundamental basketball, and a strong, firm disciplinarian. And even though I was unhappy over my brother's problems, I chose to go to Martinsville because of Curtis.

Martinsville had won its first Indiana state championship two years before, and those whom I respected claimed it was because of Curtis. Basketball was big in Martinsville. In fact, it was *the* sport. We didn't play football because it had been abolished some years before when a player was killed. And we didn't play baseball, but there was a meager track program, and I would run the dashes and broad jump once in a while, but I was no 10-flat sprinter.

Basketball dominated the life of the state and of our town. They used to say when a game was on in Martinsville, "Don't try to buy anything because everyone's at the game."

We played about twenty games in our regular season, and then we would go into the state tournament. The tournament was made up of sixty-four sectionals with sixteen teams each. Next came sixteen regionals, and then the final round of sixteen. There were no classes based on school size or player skills. The smallest or the largest school could end up champion. We were in the final championship game all of my three years at Martinsville and won the title in 1927.

The championship series can be a severe physical test. You could play four full games within a 25-hour period. For three years straight we drew the last game Friday night, the last game Saturday morning, the last game Saturday afternoon, and the championship in the final game Saturday night. It sounds horrifying, but actually, it wasn't. In those days we had the center jump rather than the end-line-in-bound pass after every basket. This gave us the opportunity to catch our breath before the jump.

I jumped center once at Martinsville in the state finals during my sophomore season. Curtis put me in for the tip against Charles (Stretch) Murphy of Marion—a big man who stood 6 feet 7 inches tall. I believe he could play today with any man of comparable size. We later played together at Purdue. My job this time was to force as tight a jump as possible so our center could block off against Murphy. The theory may have been correct but Murphy was too much. We lost to the Marion "Giants," 30–23.

During my junior year we won the state title by beating Muncie Central, 26–23. I remember that not so much for the victory but for the beautiful silver Hamilton pocket watch that the people of Martinsville gave to each of us on the team. It's a fine watch, and I keep it at home now under a little glass bell chime. It runs as well as it did the day I got it.

Usually you would think that the championship would be the important memory of my high school career. But actually, it is the defeat in the championship during my senior year that takes the honor. Again we were playing Muncie Central. With moments to go, we were ahead, 12–11. A Muncie player turned his ankle and called time out. Since they had used their allowed three times out, it was a technical foul. We had the ball when time was called. When you shot the technical, the ball went back to the center jump if you made it. I was captain and elected to refuse the shot, thereby keeping the ball. Curtis leaped off the bench yelling, "We'll shoot it, We'll shoot it."

I argued, because under the rules then, we had the ball. And by keeping it I knew that Muncie could not get it back before time ran out. I could keep it on the dribble alone and we'd win, 12–11, for back-to-back championships.

Curtis prevailed. I shot and missed, and the ball went back to the center jump. In those days, the center could tip to himself. Charlie Secrist, the Muncie center, tipped the ball behind him, grabbed it and in a wild, sweeping underhand motion arched the ball toward the basket. To this day, it is the highest arched shot I have ever seen. It seemed to go into the rafters and came straight down the middle of the basket, hardly fluttering the net.

Indiana basketball buffs still talk about that game. They'll tell you that it ended just as the ball dropped through the basket. I have personally heard the story from more people than Butler Fieldhouse could ever hold. Actually, what happened was that I called time as the ball came through the basket. Knowing Muncie would look for me to shoot, Curtis set up a play with me as the decoy. The center tipped to me, a forward screened for the center who got wide open, I faked a shot and passed to him underneath the basket, and he laid the ball up on the board. In doing so, he gave it a little English—it went around and around and around and then out. A forward was right there, but he was so confident the ball was in that he was jumping up and down in jubilation and wasn't positioned to rebound. When he saw it spin out, all he could do was bat it back up, but it didn't go in. It seemed like a disastrous turn of events at the time but by summer vacation the hurt had worn off a bit.

Hustling jobs was always a never ending task for me. Another fellow, Lloyd Whitlow, and I worked every Tuesday night at the Martinsville Elks Club. That was their dinner meeting night. We served the meal, washed the dishes, and cleaned up the kitchen. There was no guarantee, so it meant that we were dependent on tips. In passing the tray, we learned early to start with a big tipper. Usually he'd drop a dollar bill on the tray. That meant then that the others might give us a dime or a quarter instead of just a nickel or dime.

On Saturdays, I'd often box groceries at either the A & P or Kroger grocery store. I remember one Saturday night. It was just past closing time and there were a lot of loose bananas in the bin. Some of the other box boys egged me on to try and eat a dozen bananas without stopping. I ate the dozen, and instead of making me sick, it increased my appetite for them. Even today I frequently buy a banana for dessert at lunch in the Student Union.

I can't say the same about another of my eating feats. I was about six or seven and really loved my mother's coconut cream pie, I had been begging her to let me eat a whole pie. One day she did, and I haven't touched coconut pie since.

Food wasn't too expensive in those days. For five dollars you could fill the back seat of your car or wagon. But it was tough for a kid to find a job that might earn him a dollar a day.

Over the years in Martinsville, I had some fun jobs and some unusual jobs. Once I worked in the canning plant packing tomatoes and peas. Another time I worked on high tension lines planting poles in that Indiana limestone that was so soft you had to blow out the holes constantly and pop the pole in quick. I also worked on road gangs graveling county roads, using a team to haul the gravel from the pits that dot the Indiana countryside.

One of the jobs I enjoyed the most was in the Collier Brothers' Creamery. I worked with Speedy Collier on the receiving dock. We unloaded the milk, weighed each can, lifted them chest high, and poured the milk into the vat. Each full can weighed about eighty-five pounds. When you were through you were ready for a break.

In the afternoon we might work the bottling line, stack cases of bottled milk in the cooling room, or work in the ice cream plant. I remember when Eskimo Pies first came out, they were like our ice cream bars now but with no stick. We wrapped them in bright silver tinfoil.

People had always told me that when you worked in a candy store or an ice cream plant, you got tired of eating it real quick. I never did. Collier's made the greatest fresh fruit ice creams ever in the summers—strawberry, peach, blueberry, all the fresh fruit flavors. You could eat all you wanted, and in those days John Wooden didn't worry about calories or weight. He needed a lot of both.

I couldn't find any kind of a job during the summer vacation between my junior and senior years at Martinsville High. So Carl Holler, a high school friend, and I decided to hitchhike to Kansas and other midwestern states to work at harvesting wheat. Hitchhiking was tough in those days. There weren't too many cars. Most of the roads were gravel, although a few were oiled and one was bricked or paved with cement.

Everything we owned was in one suitcase. We wore our red and blue lettermen's sweater with a block "M" and stripes for years on the varsity. I had been asked by a Kansas alumnus to stop and see the late Phog Allen, then the head coach who wanted me to go to Kansas to play basketball. Then we worked two days on the KU stadium and pushed on to work the wheat harvest.

We worked fourteen to fifteen hours a day, sometimes longer, but made as much as eight dollars per day, a huge sum compared to the dollar a day we were used to in Martinsville. During the course of the summer we worked our way into the Dakotas almost to the Canadian border before heading home.

The next year, after graduating from Martinsville High, I went to work on a garbage truck in Muncie. Ball State Teachers College wanted me to go there and play basketball so they got me the job. About the second day of work, while going down a narrow alley, the truck ran over two little puppies.

"Scoop them up and throw them on," the driver told me.

"No," I said.

"If you don't throw them on, you're fired."

"I'm fired," I said. I went back to the YMCA, packed my stuff, and went down to Anderson where I got a job in the Delco-Remy factory as a buffer. On my application, the man wrote "expert buffer" under qualifications. I had never seen a buffing machine before. But there was nothing to it, and in a few days, I could do more than men who had been working there for twenty years. Then I got the word: we were paid by the hour but we also received a bonus by the piece. If we did ten pieces an hour today, they expected fifteen tomorrow and then more the next day. One day the man beside me let one of the bronze plates we were buffing slip. It sailed by his head and severed his ear. He reached down, picked up the ear and raced to the first aid station. Years later I heard they had sewed it back on and you couldn't tell the difference.

That summer also I played ball for Anderson's town team. It was here that I had one or two offers to sign a pro basketball contract. Donnie Bush, who at different times over the years managed the Senators, Pirates, White Sox, and Reds, was running the Indianapolis club in the American Association. He talked to me and so did one of his scouts. They thought I was a prospect as a shortstop, but after I hurt my arm I never could handle the deep throw from short and I was not a real good hitter. They felt I could become a good hitter, however, and that my arm would come back.

For a while I thought about signing because I enjoyed baseball so much, and the money was important, although it wasn't much by today's standards. Believe me, it was a lot more than the dollar a day I could earn in Martinsville at the creamery, and besides, it was fun.

Money was always dear to me. I worked hard for it and took great care where and how I spent it. One of the things that money was needed for, especially if you were on the basketball team, was a haircut. I always kept mine extremely short. Today you would call it a GI or a crew cut. I wore my hair that way for two reasons: it didn't have to be cut as often so you saved money, and during basketball season it never got in my eyes. It was clipped almost down to the skin, but not quite. I liked it that way, but few others did. Nellie and my mother didn't like it especially. Maybe I was just trying to assert myself; I really don't know. I'm told that there are still barbershops in Indiana where you can see the sign: "Johnny Wooden Haircuts."

5

Learn as if you were to live forever;
Live as if you were to die tomorrow.

EARLY IN LIFE, my father convinced me that the only road to success was through education. And during my junior year at Martinsville High I became aware of the fact that basketball could be the means of achieving a college education. I was always a fairly good student, and I believe I have mom and dad to thank for that.

They encouraged us to read, to study, and to learn. My lifelong interest in poetry comes from my father. He read poetry every night either before or after reading the Bible. Frequently, he read aloud to all of us. These are some of the happiest memories of my childhood.

When I was at Martinsville High there were no athletic scholarships as we know them today. About all a college or university could do for an athlete was get him a job hashing—waiting table—in a fraternity house and some kind of a weekend job to cover his tuition with a little left over for spending money.

I had four or five offers to go to college. I'd been All-State for three years, and by today's standards I was what we call a "sought-after athlete." Everett Dean, who later coached at Stanford, was then at Indiana, and he talked to me about going there. I visited Butler, where the state basketball tournament was held in Indianapolis, and talked to Tony Hinkle about playing basketball for him. George Keogan, then the basketball coach at Notre Dame came to see me, but I never visited the campus.

I had never visited Purdue or even been in West Lafayette until I entered school there in the fall of 1928. In those years, Purdue was the power in Big Ten basketball. Ward (Piggie) Lambert, who was the coach, was an impressive man and a gifted teacher but probably more important to me, he played the kind of basketball I thought I would like to play—fast break.

Coach Lambert had promised me a job waiting tables and washing dishes in the Beta house. He also thought he could get me a job on the weekends working in the athletic department handing out equipment or taping athletes in the training room. That paid thirty-five cents an hour—big money to me in those days.

With all my belongings in one suitcase and a dollar or two in my pocket, some friends drove me to West Lafayette where I hoped to be good enough to play basketball and smart enough to get my degree.

That first semester, I discovered that if a student made the Dean's list he got free tuition for the spring semester. From then on, I worked especially hard to make honor roll. As I recall, tuition was about seventy-five dollars a semester. And when you divide that by thirty-five cents an hour, it meant putting in a lot of hours just to pay tuition.

During basketball season, I only worked breakfast and lunch in the fraternity house because I was at practice during the dinner hour. I had to eat later and then clean off the table, do the dishes, and police up the kitchen. Then I could begin to study for the grades to keep me on the free tuition roster.

I think I had more jobs in my four years at Purdue than anyone could possibly imagine.

Stretch Murphy, the great Purdue center, "willed" to me the program concession for the basketball games. I got the starting line-ups and numerical roster for both teams and had them mimeographed with the up-to-date statistics of the teams and players. Then I'd get some high school kids in West Lafayette to sell them at the game for a dime apiece. They made a nickel, and I made a nickel. I don't recall how much I'd clear, but it was only a few dollars.

Now, football programs were different. I sold them for four years. Early on a Friday morning I would get five hundred programs checked out to me, and I'd make the hotels and restaurants where the alumni were hanging out. I soon learned to time myself so as to catch them when they were feeling pretty good from an over-exposure to bootleg liquor. If they were especially "happy," instead of getting a dime for a program, my take could range all the way from a quarter to a dollar. Selling football programs helped me accumulate a little money for books and supplies and a date with Nellie when I could get back to Martinsville.

It was always a scramble to try to figure out ways to make a little more money. One of the most unusual was my "walk to Chicago." I bought the concession rights on the special football train that ran on the Monon Railroad from Lafayette to Chicago. One of the Big Ten's most famous rivalries then was between Purdue and Chicago. Amos Alonzo Stagg was the head coach of Chicago, and, next to Knute Rockne, he was probably the most famous name in football.

I hired a couple of my frat brothers to work with me, and we would walk up and down the aisles hawking our wares as the train rolled toward Chicago and onto a special siding near the university. We'd sell sandwiches, candy, cigarettes, chewing gum, apples, oranges, and soft drinks. It was hard work walking up and down those aisles, and it took a lot of hustling to get things together to sell that would make a profit.

Coach Lambert believed an athlete should work for his education. Then it would be appreciated more. I remember during my sophomore year he called me into his office. It was near the start of the season for my first year of varsity competition. Coach Lambert told me that there was a doctor in Lafayette who had taken a liking to me and wanted to pay my way through Purdue so I wouldn't have to work so hard. "He'll pay your fraternity house bill, your fees, tuition, and anything else you may need."

"That's wonderful, coach," I told him.

"Are you going to take it, John?"

"What do you mean?"

"I just wonder how you're going to pay him back."

"Coach," I said, "I thought you just told me that he wanted to do it."

"That is right, John, he does. Remember, though, that I told you when you came to Purdue, you would work hard but would get through and wouldn't owe me or anyone else a cent. You will have earned your way.

"Now if you accept this doctor's offer, even though he doesn't expect to be repaid, I think you're the kind of person who wouldn't feel right about it unless you did.

"Think about it, John," he said, "and in a day or two I'll talk to you again."

A couple of days later, I went by to see him. "I decided not to accept the doctor's offer."

"I really didn't think you would, John," he said, "after you thought about it."

Later on he called me in again and said that the same doctor would like to give me a suit and a topcoat. Coach Lambert felt I should accept this, and I did. It was the second suit I ever owned. I got my first suit for my graduation from high school, and I had never owned a topcoat.

My last year at Purdue was the most dedicated of all. I worked at every possible job, at the same time studying hard to make the Dean's list. There was little time for anything but basketball, books, work and, once in a while, pool, which I'd learned to play pretty well in Martinsville.

Nellie and I had seemed destined for each other from our first meeting. Even in high school we were sure that we would one day marry, but Nellie insisted that I go to Purdue and that she would wait those long years. Thus, it came as a shock to her during the summer between my junior and senior years that I had an offer to leave Purdue and accept an appointment to the United States Military Academy at West Point.

Back in those years, West Point was allowed to recruit as cadets proficient athletes who had graduated from college and play them another four years. One of Purdue's great football players, a fullback named Elmer Oliphant, went to West Point after graduating. Another great Army back, Chris Cagle, had done the same thing.

A uniform must have had some allure for me since in high school I had joined an infantry unit of the local National Guard. But when I told Nellie about the offer there was what you would call a confrontation.

"I agreed to wait these four years," she told me. "You go, but I'll wait no longer."

That ended my consideration of West Point and began our planning to be married upon my graduation from Purdue. It was a big step for us, the biggest of our lives. It required advance planning and a forced saving program as neither of our parents had the means to provide financial assistance. However, they gave us the kind of love and guidance for which we consider ourselves to be very fortunate.

After the close of the Big Ten season and a second championship, I received an offer from George Halas, the man who created and coached the Chicago Bears football team for so many years. Halas, who also owned a basketball team then, hired me to come to Chicago and play three games for a hundred dollars each, the most money I had ever had in one lump sum in my life. There probably was considerable interest in my playing since Purdue had won the Big Ten title, and I had made All-American for the third year, in the process breaking Stretch Murphy's conference scoring record with 154 points in the twelve games. In addition I had been selected as College Player of the Year.

In Chicago, I met Frank Kautsky for whom I later played pro basketball on weekends and in the summers during many years of my coaching career in Indiana.

At the same time a representative of the original New York Celtics approached me about joining the team to barnstorm around the country. They offered me five thousand dollars for the year, an unheard-of figure to me, as some teachers who also coached were making as little as nine hundred dollars a year. Eighteen hundred dollars was considered a fine salary.

The Celtic offer seemed tremendous. Once again, I went to Piggie Lambert about it.

"What did you come to Purdue for?" he asked, after hearing me out.

"To get an education," I told him.

"Did you get one?"

"I think so."

"You're not going to use it?" he asked.

"I hope to."

"Well, you won't be using it barnstorming around the country playing basketball. You're not that type of person."

Purdue had offered me a teaching fellowship in English upon graduation. I weighed that quite carefully but Coach Lambert, in his way, had convinced me that coaching was the best direction to take. By the time the spring semester of my senior year was ended, Nellie and I had set our wedding date, and I had a job at Dayton, Kentucky, as athletic director, coach, and teacher.

We were going to be married August 8, 1932. That was a Sunday. I had saved 909 dollars and a nickel from barnstorming games around Indiana, Illinois, Ohio, and Kentucky during the spring and summer after the end of my senior season. We had ordered a brand new Plymouth sedan and would take delivery on Saturday.

That morning when I went to the First Bank and Trust Company to withdraw a part of the $909.05, it wasn't open. The bank had gone broke.

Immediately, we canceled the order for the Plymouth and the wedding. We had planned to be married in Indianapolis in a quiet little church ceremony because Nellie's father wasn't well and couldn't afford a large wedding. Furthermore, the minister in Indianapolis had married Nellie's only brother, Emil, to her sister-in-law, Julia.

To say we were despondent that Saturday hardly expresses our feelings—we were totally depressed. That $909.05 seemed like our lives that day. Even so, we knew we were more fortunate than many elderly people who had lost their life savings. We were young and could bounce back.

When the word of the bank failure and our wedding plans got to the father of Nellie's best friend, Mary Schnaiter, he called me immediately. Mr. Schnaiter, who owned a large grain mill in Martinsville, offered to lend me two hundred dollars to be paid back when I could so Nellie and I could be married. Though it was and still is against my principles to borrow from anyone, we did accept the loan. My brother Cat and his wife-to-be drove us to Indianapolis and stood up for us.

After the little ceremony, we went to dinner at the Bamboo Inn in Indianapolis and to the Circle theater to hear the Mills Brothers. We have kidded about that show for years. The Mills Brothers answered encore after encore and they have remained my favorite singing group.

The next morning we had to get up early. Coach Lambert was giving a basketball clinic in Vincennes, a city in southern Indiana, and was driving by Martinsville to pick me up. I was going to get $25—a very vital $25 since the loss of the $909.05—for being part of that week-long clinic.

At 6:00 A.M. we caught the bus out of Indianapolis back to Martinsville where I left Nellie for that first week while I participated in the clinic. We were probably one of very few couples to have spent their first week of marriage apart.

6

The true athlete should have character, not be a character.

A GREAT MANY people are responsible for my success in basketball, both as a player and a coach. Nellie, who waited through the Purdue years so we could marry, was the most important person spiritually and mentally. She kept me going during many dark hours.

From a technician's viewpoint, however, Coach Piggie Lambert has had the greatest influence on my career both from the viewpoint of playing as well as coaching.

There has never been any doubt in my mind that Lambert was definitely way ahead of his time. A comparatively small man, Lambert was a fine athlete. He had gone to Wabash College in Indiana, was a quarterback on its football team in a historic game with Notre Dame, played professional baseball, and was a thorough student of basketball.

A dynamic, fiery individual, Lambert was known throughout the Midwest as a brilliant, free-lance strategist whose teams were always prepared mentally and physically.

It was from Lambert that I first realized the value of a controlled offense with free-lance aspects. In other words, Lambert believed in building a platform or a base from which the offense would start. He wanted movement by design but not by precise, repeated pattern.

There was always someone going in, going out, and crossing over. Within this platform he would design little improvised changes that capitalized on the individual abilities of his team. When he had Stretch Murphy playing center during my sophomore year, we did it a little differently than when Dutch Fehring, who once coached the line at UCLA and at Stanford, was the post man.

Lambert was not set in his ways. If the guards seemed superior he might utilize them more. He always went to the strength of the individuals after studying each of us closely. Lambert was a great psychologist, accomplishing more with words than any coach I've ever known. I think it is one of my attributes that can definitely be traced to him. He was not one for team meetings; I'm not either.

Every day in practice, he might stop you several times and point out that you are going too much to your right or too much to your left. He always had options, as he never wanted to take away a man's initiative; he merely wanted to direct it within the bounds of his attack.

Coach Lambert never gave you a demand route. He might say, "The first two times you hit the center, fake right and go left. The third time, reverse it. You must outthink, outmaneuver, and outcondition your opponent."

Players had tremendous respect for him. He worked hard and expected you to work hard. It is because of his theory on condition that I have based my entire coaching career on a similar thesis. Lambert brought this point home early in my years with him.

On one occasion we were to play Indiana. Everett Dean, one of the fine coaches, was then at Indiana. But Coach Lambert told us we could beat them.

"We'll beat them because Mr. Dean is too nice a person. He will not work his players hard enough for them to stay with us. We'll wear them down in the first three quarters of the game and beat them in the last quarter.

You see, we're prepared to run the whole game, but Indiana isn't."

If any one premise typifies my teams in all the years I've coached, it is this concept, Often as a player, I'd tell myself, "I may play someone better than I am, but I'll never run against one who is going to be in better condition." And I never played against a man in my life I felt was in better shape, and Lambert often cited me as an example of top conditioning.

But there is considerable difference between Lambert's theory on conditioning a team and mine. He believed in continual full court, up and down, work. He might scrimmage a team an hour the day before a game, but I never do. Also, he scrimmaged five on five a lot more than I do. It seems to me that I achieve the same conditioning with a lot more two-on-two, three-on-three drills, and five-on-five half-court situations.

While I try to achieve my aims through these drills, Lambert accomplished a similar purpose within a full court, five-on-five scrimmage. Basically, our coaching concept sought the same result; we just went down different streets.

Lambert constantly urged us not to worry about our opponent—just play our own game and force him to follow it. We were made to believe that those of us playing for him at Purdue were the best in basketball. Confidence was a virtue he attempted to exploit at all times.

In all probability Coach Meanwell of Wisconsin was one of the finest pattern basketball coaches in the country. He used a weave offense almost continuously. When we played them, we would press the ball at what would now be the mid-court line. We'd press them tight, and when they were through running their weave, instead of being under the basket, we had forced them to finish up twenty or twenty-five feet out. Lambert insisted that they would never deviate, never change, but I worried constantly about Wisconsin going to reverses on us and coming back to our weak side.

As the only starter back in my junior year and captain of the team, and thoroughly indoctrinated into all the Lambert principles, I felt that I could speak up.

"Mr. Lambert," I asked, "don't you think we're leaving ourselves vulnerable to reverses by pressing so tight against Wisconsin?"

"Yes, we are," he responded, "but Meanwell has his players drilled and coached so well in his offense that they'll never try to reverse." His method was to force them out of what they wanted to do, and then they'd break down. It worked all the time. Wisconsin never really hurt us with reverses, even though we were very vulnerable.

In the past few years following our great success at UCLA, I have overheard people say that I originated the pressing defense. Not at all. I played the press at Purdue under Lambert. It wasn't a zone press, but it was a pressing defense with zone principles. At that time I didn't know of any other coach using it.

The press works in so naturally with the fast break offense. The foremost exponent of fast break basketball was Piggie Lambert. He believed in speed, and that the team which made the most mistakes would probably win. Now, that statement takes a bit of analyzing. What he was trying to get across was that the doer makes mistakes, but the doer usually wins because he gets more shots and controls the game more.

Actually, if there was an originator of fast break basketball, it was Lambert. He demanded movement and action. I admonish my boys with a different verb—move, move. I want movement. In the end we both want the same.

Lambert was also a very precise man. Known as a man who thought of everything, he was meticulous, thorough, and well organized. And while conditioning and organization were two of Lambert's demands, one thing he couldn't control was accidents. I probably had more accidents in my four years of college than anyone. Just before the Christmas holidays of my freshman year, I came down with scarlet fever and spent three weeks in isolation.

Then, in my sophomore season we were leaving to play Butler in Indianapolis. Andrew Thomas, whose nickname was "Prune," and I were waiting for the trolley that ran between West Lafayette and Lafayette. After a time we discovered that the trolley couldn't make it to where we were because of ice on the track. So when a fellow we knew came by driving a small truck and motioned us to climb into the back end, we jumped at the chance. I was carrying my basketball gear and a Christmas present for Nellie. Prune climbed up ahead of me, and I tossed our gear up to him and was trying to pull myself up with one hand while holding Nellie's gift with the other.

"Watch out," yelled Prune.

I whirled around just in time to see a truck bearing down on us. It couldn't stop because of the ice. I tried to swing out of the way, but it was too late. I was caught between the two trucks, and a rod protruding from one of the trucks jammed right through my thigh. Nellie's present—a little vanity case—was shattered, and I spent that Christmas in the hospital.

The next year, just before the holidays, I was at practice and cut sharply on a drive off the post man. Slipping on a loose plank, I crashed to the floor and gouged out a hunk of flesh. Blood was spurting all over the place, and I was rushed to the hospital again for what I thought would be just a day or two. However, infection set in, and I spent another Christmas in the hospital.

To make it all complete, in my senior year Lambert was disturbed because I kept getting an infected throat. Just before the holidays, it cleared up and he suggested I have a tonsillectomy. Another Christmas—four in a row—in the hospital.

In all probability, however, it was the injury during my sophomore year that was the most damaging. Not only did it shatter Nellie's gift but Lambert always insisted that we would have remained unbeaten if I hadn't tried to hop that truck. He claimed that my being out caused the team to lose its tempo even though Murphy and the rest were in the game.

Today, only the real basketball buffs who lived in the Midwest are aware of just how great Stretch Murphy was. He's in the Hall of Fame. In my opinion, he was an all-time great player. Stretch was the first really big man to play basketball with coordination and skill. He was quick and could jump. His timing was flawless, and he was a great rebounder and shooter. In addition, Stretch was a great team player.

There is no doubt that it was Murphy who started me on my way to being an outstanding player. I might not have become so well known if I hadn't played with him as a sophomore. His presence and Lambert's coaching insured our having a great team.

We both made All-American during my sophomore year. And I've always contended that if you make it as a sophomore, it's not as hard to make it again as a junior and senior, as I did. It was during my senior year that I broke Stretch's Big Ten scoring record.

Over the years since I graduated, I've wondered how we would have done in an NCAA tournament as it is constituted now. Those tournaments are packed with pressure. It's sudden death, and there's little room for a mistake. Lambert was a man who made a fetish out of stressing little details, and I am sure that if we'd had the opportunity, we would have done well.

I think most of us have a superstition or a fetish that becomes part of life. I had one as a player, although I don't believe I'm a superstitious person. But if you look at any photograph taken of me at Purdue, you will notice a key tied into the lace on my left shoe.

Why?

At first it seemed a very practical purpose. We didn't have combination locks then, and there were no pockets in basketball uniforms. So, I just ran the lace through the hole in the key to my locker, then double tied the lace. After a time some sports writer noticed it and called it a "good luck" piece. Actually, it had nothing to do with luck but was merely a handy place to keep the key.

During my senior year, I was pretty close to Lambert. Since I was the only senior and had started for three years, I knew what he wanted done on the floor, and by then I was reasonably certain that I wanted to become a coach. I had achieved the closeness that exists between player and coach, although at the time I wasn't truly aware of it.

We had a fine team my senior season, losing only one game all year, and that was to Illinois. There was a bit of irony in that defeat. We were driving to Champaign-Urbana for the game in Lambert's car. On an icy stretch of highway outside of Champaign we rolled over. Glass broke and I cut my right hand rather deeply.

I played despite the cuts but really couldn't do too much. Whether we would have won if we hadn't had the accident we'll never know. But I did lead the Big Ten in scoring that year, and in that game I was well below average.

It just seemed, looking back, that I must have been accident-prone, especially where cars and trucks were involved.

7

Do not let what you cannot do interfere with what you can do.

MY FIRST coaching assignment at Dayton High was filled with foreboding. Nellie's sister, Audrey, and her husband, Ray, drove us down from Martinsville. We didn't have a car because my money was still tied up in the bank foreclosure, and it appeared we were never going to see a penny of it again. Everything we owned was either in the trunk or on the back seat of their car.

We had no place to live, no furniture and no personal things except for our clothes and a few wedding gifts. The superintendent of schools, Olin W. Davis, hired me for $1800 per year, a fine salary for those days. He helped us find an apartment and arranged for us to buy furniture on time. The people who lived in the apartment below us, Melvin and Dorothybell Wuest, are still dear friends.

The assignment in Dayton was rather horrifying when I look back on it. My precise duties included athletic director, head football coach, head basketball coach, head baseball coach, head track coach, supervisor of the total physical education curriculum from the first through the twelfth grade, plus teaching English.

Only football worried me. Since Martinsville didn't have a team, I had never played the game. And I hadn't tried it at Purdue, even as a freshman. During the summer before school started I had spent many hours with Purdue's head coach, Noble Kizer, and his assistant, Mal Elward. Both were fine technicians and knew the game, but you don't learn football with talks and diagrams. It was obvious at the outset that it was unfair to the Dayton players for John Wooden to continue something for which he was not qualified.

After explaining this to Mr. Davis, I asked to be relieved and suggested that Willard Bass, who had been football coach prior to my acceptance, should resume the assignment, and I would help where I could. Davis agreed, and Bass took over. We had a good season, losing only one game, and some record books still list John Wooden as head football coach.

It has been said over the years that I haven't had a losing season in basketball since I began at Dayton, but that isn't so. I can't recall the figures, but we lost more than we won during my first season. Things picked up in my second year, and we had a fine team, closing out the season with only three or four defeats.

On weekends I played pro basketball for the Kautsky Athletic Club. We played thirty to forty games a year throughout the Midwest. I got fifty dollars a game plus an expense allowance for travel. Frank Kautsky was a marvelous man, a true basketball buff, and when we won or had a good game, he would see that we got a little bonus in our envelope after the game.

In all I played pro ball, primarily for Kautsky, for about six years. It was during my last year that the center jump was abolished. I've always thought that it would have been great to have played my entire career under those new rules. The year after the center jump was eliminated I scored twice as much as I had ever scored before even though I had slipped some because of a leg injury. The game without the center jump was right up my alley.

I remember one year when I was playing for Kautsky that I made 100 consecutive free throws. When the 100th dropped through the basket, Kautsky stopped the game and gave me a hundred dollar bill. It was the first time I had ever seen a hundred dollar bill. Believe me, Nellie grabbed that in a hurry.

There wasn't a pro basketball league at that time, so we played in places like Indianapolis, Ft. Wayne, Sheboygan, Oshkosh, Chicago, Detroit, and Akron. Usually the teams were sponsored by a large plant such as Goodyear or Firestone or by someone like Frank Kautsky.

One of the great teams we played those years was the New York Rens. I guess you could call them the forerunners of the Harlem Globetrotters. The greatest pure shooter I ever faced was one of their players, Bill Yancey. Fats Jenkins, a guard who also played outfield with the New York Black Yankees, was another gifted player and a fine person. And their center, Wee Willie Smith, was the toughest, meanest basketball player I ever faced. He wasn't dirty, just tough and mean. We met again years later at the basketball Hall of Fame. I always contended that Willie could have whipped Joe Louis, who was heavyweight champion then, if he had been a boxer. He weighed about 220, had a beautiful build, was quick, with lightning reflexes, had great balance, and was truly a superb athlete.

Pro basketball in those days was hectic and harrowing. Even the stories that are told about the early years of the NBA couldn't compare to my years when we carried our own gear, liniment, tape, bandages, and basketball. It was a life all its own and was certainly different from the life of an average Indiana school teacher.

Midway during my second year in Dayton, I was offered a position in the South Bend, Indiana, school system. It meant returning to my home state, being in a larger school, and living in a bigger city. And in addition, South Bend was the home of Notre Dame. I had enjoyed Dayton, the people, the school, the kids, and especially O. W. Davis, the superintendent, who had hired me. Also, our daughter, Nancy, had been born in nearby Covington. So, we had many attachments to the Dayton area, but now, in the summer of 1934, it was back to Indiana. This time we moved in our own Plymouth, plus a moving van. We'd acquired a few more possessions as well as a daughter.

Nellie was more content back in Indiana. And South Bend Central High presented a tremendous challenge to a young coach in one of the toughest high school conferences in the country.

I was the athletic director, basketball and baseball coach, the tennis coach, taught some English classes, and later on was comptroller of the school. This was rather ironic. I am not too good a numbers man, and I certainly don't claim to be a professional businessman. It was a good thing that I had such fine assistants as Mrs. Clara McClary, C. L. Kuhn, and Walt Kindy.

Being the comptroller meant I was responsible for the book store, the cafeteria, and the ticket sales to all school events, athletic or otherwise. I'll always remember what happened one time after our annual football game with Mishawaka, the next town just east of South Bend. That game was played in the Notre Dame stadium. We almost filled it a time or two, and, if I'm not mistaken, student tickets were a quarter, advance adult tickets were fifty cents, and all gate sale tickets were a dollar.

There were many places around South Bend that sold advance tickets. After the game was over on Saturday, I'd make my rounds with my little black satchel and pick up the unsold tickets and the money for those that had been sold in advance.

Looking back on those collection rounds, I can see that it was foolish to handle it that way. I could easily have been robbed or have misplaced a collection or two and then I would have been in bad trouble.

I was bonded, and insured, of course, but probably would have resisted any hold-up attempt. One time I was in my office balancing out the collections. Everything was in and tabulated carefully, but I was twenty dollars short. I went back over all my addition and checked the beginning and ending number on all the ticket rolls, but I was still short.

Usually when this happened, I would go over it with

greater care and find where I had made my error, but this time I found no error. I knew it had to be something simple because it was an even amount. By this time I had been through the brown envelopes at least two or three times. But once again, I fingered through the envelopes and there in the one from Clark's Restaurant was a twenty dollar bill. The glue in the bottom of the envelope had become wet and the bill had stuck to it.

There never seemed to be a dull day at Central. I enjoyed the school, the city, the people, and the players. Central did well in both basketball and baseball during my years. We won the conference many times but never took the state championship. We didn't have much luck in the state tournament or in any one-game, sudden death tournament, such as the NCAA.

We had some happy years in South Bend. Our son, Jim, was born there. And I believe to this day that if World War II hadn't come along to take me away in 1943, that I would still be at Central High. We weren't getting wealthy, but we had a wonderful life, a fine school, great associates, and I always felt I was cut out for the high school level. I loved to teach, and I lived for it. Furthermore, a teacher could not ask for a finer principal under whom to work than Mr. P. D. Pointer.

As a matter of fact, I'm frequently asked why I chose coaching as a career and then stayed with it. Amos Alonzo Stagg, who coached football at Chicago when I used to make my annual "walk to Chicago," best sums up my feelings on the subject. Stagg, who worked with youth and coached well into his nineties, when asked why he coached once said, "It was because of a promise I made to God."

As a young man, Stagg planned to become a minister and attended Yale Theological School. One day after talking with God through prayer he decided he could best serve Him on the athletic field rather than from the pulpit. He once wrote, "I have made the young men of America my ministry. I have tried to bring out the best in the boys that I have coached. I truly believe that many of them have become better Christians and citizens because of what they have learned on the athletic field.

"You must love your boys to get the most out of them and do the most for them. I have worked with boys whom I haven't admired, but I have loved them just the same. Love has dominated my coaching career as I am sure it has and always will that of many other coaches and teachers."

I feel that my love for young people is the main reason I have stayed in coaching and have refused positions that would have been far more lucrative.

A poem by Glennice L. Harmon that ran many years ago in the *NEA Journal* typifies my deep feelings on the subject:*

THEY ASK ME WHY I TEACH

> They ask me why I teach,
> And I reply,
> Where could I find more splendid company?
> There sits a statesman,
> Strong, unbiased, wise,
> Another later Webster,
> Silver-tongued.
> And there a doctor
> Whose quick, steady hand
> Can mend a bone,
> Or stem the lifeblood's flow.
> A builder sits beside him—
> Upward rise
> The arches of a church he builds, wherein
> That minister will speak the word of God,
> And lead a stumbling soul to touch the Christ.
>
> And all about
> A lesser gathering

---

* "They Ask Me Why I Teach," by Glennice L. Harmon, in *NEA Journal* 37, no. 1 (September 1948): 375.

Of farmers, merchants, teachers,
Laborers, men
Who work and vote and build
And plan and pray
Into a great tomorrow.
And I say,
"I may not see the church,
Or hear the word,
Or eat the food their hands will grow."
And yet—I may.
And later I may say,
"I knew the lad,
And he was strong,
Or weak, or kind, or proud,
Or bold, or gay.
I knew him once,
But then he was a boy."
They ask me why I teach, and I reply,
"Where could I find more splendid company?"

8

*You cannot live a perfect day
    without doing something for someone
Who will never be able to repay you.*

I OFTEN TELL my players that next to my own flesh and blood, they are the closest to me. They are my children. I get wrapped up in them, their lives, and their problems.

Sometimes this concern for my players becomes so dominant that it is quite possible that it may subconsciously influence decisions that I may have to make in regard to personnel. I try to be fair and give each player the treatment he earns and deserves, but realize that I may be subconsciously influenced at times.

Although I strive constantly to avoid this, one exception stands out in my memory. It was at South Bend Central. I had a fine second baseman on my baseball team who was also a guard on the basketball team, but he had never done well in basketball practice and it's always been my premise to give the ones who do best in practice the vast majority of the playing time in the games.

On this particular weekend during his junior year at Central, we were playing Emerson of Gary on Friday, and the next night we were to play Fort Wayne Central. We edged Emerson by a point or two and were driving back to South Bend from Gary. We had stopped in a restaurant to eat, and everyone was sitting together in the luxury of a big win when I noticed Eddie Pawelski all alone in a corner.

"What's the matter, Eddie?" I asked.

"I don't get to play, coach, so I'm thinking about quitting."

"You know, Eddie, I don't like quitters. You shouldn't quit. You should stick it out." My advice might well have been based on the fact that I didn't want to lose him for basketball because I might also lose him for baseball, and I expected a lot from him for the next two baseball seasons.

"Coach," he said, "I know I can play ball if I just had a chance. If I could just get in there with Eddie Ehlers, Jimmy Powers, Warren Seaborg, and the other players, I know I can do well playing with them."

I thought that I'd just shut him up real quick. "All right, Eddie," I said, "I'll give you a chance. I'll start you against Fort Wayne Central tomorrow night."

Suddenly I wondered where those words came from. Three of us were locked in a battle for No. 1 in Indiana. We had just beaten Emerson and tomorrow we faced powerful Fort Wayne Central. Murray Mendenhall, who later coached in the original NBA, was at Fort Wayne, and his team was built around Bill Armstrong who later became an All-American at Indiana University and was truly a great player.

Eddie hadn't played in the Emerson game. In fact, he hadn't played much in any game because he looked so bad. Yet, here I was going into a crucial game and I'd just told him he could start when he wasn't even a number two guard—actually I think he was number five.

As we drove home to South Bend, I told Nellie that I'd made a horrible mistake. "I told Eddie Pawelski I'd start him tomorrow night, and now I have to go through with it."

To this day I've never figured out why I did that. I do not believe appeasement is best for either party. I try never to compromise my judgment because of my affection for a boy. Decisions must be based on reason, not emotion.

"Well," Nellie replied, "you never said how long you'd play him, did you?"

"No, I didn't. I just said I'd start him."

The next night I started Eddie against Fort Wayne. I figured I'd shut him up within a minute or two because I just knew he'd play up to his practice performance and that would be so embarrassing for him before a large crowd that he would be happy when I replaced him.

I put Eddie on Armstrong, the toughest player in the state. Eddie literally took him apart. Armstrong got the lowest point total of his career, Eddie scored 12, and our team showed the best balance of all season. Actually, I don't think Eddie had ever scored 12 points total in his entire career. But in addition to his scoring, his defense, rebounding, and play-making were excellent.

Eddie never sat on the bench again except to rest. He started every game and was named the most valuable player that year and again the following year as a senior. He went on to Indiana University and I warned Coach Branch McCracken that he'd be the poorest practice player he ever had but he could be a great game player if given the opportunity.

Indiana never got to see Eddie play. World War II broke out and he enlisted in the service. Ultimately, he came with me to Indiana State. Because of an injury he couldn't play and became my assistant and later came to UCLA with me. By then he had changed his name to Eddie Powell. After a couple years at UCLA he became head coach at Loyola of Los Angeles, then moved into city government work and is now city manager of Placentia, a suburb of Los Angeles.

Why I ever said I would start him is still a mystery to me. I've had other kids come to me many times since and ask the same question, but I've never appeased one since—at least in that respect. Perhaps there was another Eddie Powell among those kids. I'll never know.

Every once in a while, though, I think back to that restaurant in Indiana and that brief exchange with Eddie. He was one of my favorites, there is no doubt about it. Perhaps unknowingly I had compromised my better judgment because of my personal feelings, or perhaps because I wanted him happy for the baseball season, a sport of which I am very fond.

There was another youngster at Central of whom I was also very fond and who, in his way, got to me. That was Harvey Martin, a kid from the wrong side of the tracks, a tough competitor, and a real fine ball player, but he constantly caused problems.

For several days at practice, Harvey had created a disturbance by arguing with another player, Wayne Thompson. Wayne's father was a professor of law at Notre Dame. Harvey seemed to think that Wayne was a sissy. It is true that Wayne was not hard-nosed like Harvey, but he still could handle things pretty well.

On this particular day, Harvey was interrupting practice by badgering Wayne. I had talked to both of their fathers about the problem and had told them my proposed solution. The fathers supported my proposal and I decided to try it.

The idea was to put them into the boxing ring one day right during practice. At the time we worked out at the YMCA in South Bend and the ring was on the way up to the basketball floor.

"We're going to settle this once and for all," I told both of them as I stopped practice.

"We're going to put you two in the ring with the old-fashioned rules—no three-minute round, no bell. If some one goes down, we'll stop things to see if he wants to continue. If you don't go down, I don't want any running around. Mix it up and get it over with."

Harvey was in his glory. He was a rough, tough street fighter, but in the ring it was a different story. Wayne could hold his own. Harvey came rushing out of his corner and drew back to throw one from the bleacher seats.

Wayne just slipped the punch and popped a left in his face and Harvey sat down hard. He wasn't hurt, but he was stunned and surprised. A trickle of blood came from his nose, but he hopped right up ready to go, obviously embarrassed.

Harvey rushed bull fashion at Wayne again, but this time he was more cautious. Wayne faked a shot, and Harvey covered his face with both hands. Thompson crossed with his right to the pit of Harvey's stomach.

This time Harvey went down hard, rolling around and gasping for breath. I gave him some smelling salts and said, "Are you satisfied?"

"Naw, I'd like one more chance."

Once more he barged in. Wayne set him up with a fake or two and dropped him again. When I went over to check him, he rolled over and breathed deeply of smelling salts.

"Are you convinced, Harvey?" I asked.

"Yep, I barked up the wrong tree."

It wasn't until later that Harvey found out that Wayne's father had boxed at the University of Michigan and that Wayne was a proficient boxer. After that Harvey would always warn a potential problem-maker with, "You'd better behave. I'll get Wayne after you."

They became good friends, and while I have never done that before or since, it solved the problem once and for all.

One of the real pleasures of coaching is the association you build up with kids like this. You follow a good many of them the rest of your life, and their joys and disappointments become your joys and disappointments. You love to see them excel in whatever profession they pursue.

There's a community leader by the name of Eddie Ehlers in South Bend today who played for me at Central and who fits that mold. He was probably as gifted an all-around athlete as I have ever seen.

He was so skilled as a Purdue fullback that he was a high draft pick of the Chicago Bears. Eddie was also selected by the Boston Celtics in the NBA, but the New York Yankees signed him to a fine bonus contract. However, he also played some with the Boston Celtics.

My introduction to Ehlers came one spring when baseball practice was rained out, and we were in the gym playing pick-up basketball. The junior high basketball prospects who were entering Central the next year would always show up when it rained in the spring because they knew that I would call off baseball practice and have basketball practice.

Eddie was a tremendous prospect. It was only a question of which sport—football, basketball, track, or baseball. On this particular day during a break Eddie came up to me and said, "Coach, every time I make a basket I look over at you and you're shaking your head no at me. My junior high coach would always nod his head and smile when I scored."

"Eddie," I said, "why are you looking at me after a basket? Don't you have someone to guard? I don't want you looking at me, and I don't want you looking up at the stands. You can be sure that I'll always shake my head as long as you're playing for the plaudits of the coach and the crowd."

He looked at me kind of hurt, but he never turned his eyes toward me again in the years he played for me at Central. He was always looking to pick up his man. However, he did draw many a smile and many a pat on the back from me.

Years later, Eddie stopped by Terre Haute to see me one day. By now he was in the Yankee chain playing for Quincy, Illinois, in the Three-Eye-League. Eddie was all confidence. He was a handsome young man, intelligent, and a great athlete. After talking for a few minutes, he said, "Coach, do you mind if I call you John?"

"No, Eddie, I think that would be fine."

A gleam of accomplishment crossed his eye. I could see he was pleased.

"Well, John, it's like this," he continued, "I'm doing pretty well, John. I've signed for a big baseball bonus, John. I got a good salary, John, with the Celtics last winter, and you probably think I'm on a Three-Eye-League salary.

"I'm not. I probably make more money than you do, John. That's why I think I should call you John. Don't you think so, John? Don't you agree, John?"

During the next five minutes he called me John a dozen times. Then suddenly he stopped. "I can't do it," he said. "I've tried. It's going to have to be coach."

9

*Be more concerned with your character,
than with your reputation,
Because your character is what you
really are
While your reputation is merely
what others think you are.*

WHEN PEARL HARBOR WAS attacked on December 7, 1941, I had been at South Bend Central about seven years. I tried immediately to get into service and finally enlisted in 1942. However, I wasn't called to active duty until February of 1943. Induction into an officer's training program was to take me away from South Bend, coaching, and my other duties until 1946.

My first assignment as a lieutenant, junior grade, was at the University of North Carolina in Chapel Hill. There I found myself surrounded by a large group of men who had all been connected with athletics as coaches or players. We were to undergo a 30-day period of indoctrination to prepare us for the Naval Air Corps V-5 physical fitness program.

One of my roommates was the late Paul Christman, the former Missouri All-American and pro quarterback with the Chicago Cardinals. Most people probably remember him from his career as a commentator on pro football telecasts. Paul, a delightful man, was so far advanced in naval training that he made the rest of us look like apprentice seamen. He owed his superiority to having gone through basic training as a seaman at Great Lakes Naval Training Station prior to being assigned to officer's training.

Our group also included Bud Wilkinson, who later became one of the great coaches at Oklahoma and is now a TV commentator for college football; the late Jim Tatum, who gained coaching fame at North Carolina and Maryland after the war; and Don Faurot, who developed Paul Christman at Missouri. That's also where I met the late Red Sanders, who did so much to develop UCLA into a major national football power before his death.

Following the thirty days at Chapel Hill, I was assigned to Iowa Pre-Flight on the campus of the University of Iowa at Iowa City. Within less than ninety days, I received orders to report to the U.S.S. Franklin, somewhere in the South Pacific, as a fitness officer.

After a short leave—which I spent in South Bend—I was enroute back to Iowa City to close out my affairs when I became quite ill. Stubbornly ignoring the severe pains in my side, I pushed on into Iowa City and the Navy residence area at the university. The doctor who checked me over at sick bay told me I had a red-hot appendix and they would have to operate right away.

Since Navy regulations say you can't go to sea for a minimum of thirty days after certain types of surgery, my orders to the Franklin were rewritten. I was reassigned to Iowa Pre-Flight and a friend of mine from Purdue, Freddie Stalcup, replaced me on the Franklin. Perhaps it was coincidence that Freddie, a Purdue fraternity brother and football player, and I were look-alikes. His battle station on the Franklin was the gun position that was hit by a kamikaze, resulting in the terrible fire that virtually destroyed the Franklin. But for the emergency appendectomy that seemed so unfortunate when it happened, John Wooden's name rather than Freddie Stalcup's would probably have been on the casualty list of dead.

A series of assignments followed, including one at St. Simons Island, Georgia, where ironically, since I don't drink, I had the responsibility for the officers' wine mess. Counting cases of bourbon, scotch, and gin bore only remote resemblance to the football and basketball tickets I had handled as comptroller at South Bend Central.

All of my players have heard my lecture on the subject of drinking. I explain the problems it can create for them, the university and for me. I hope that they have sufficient pride in our program that they will refrain for the few months of basketball, but realize that liquor is so often present in the home today that you must use reason with regulations. There was a time in my coaching career when drinking or smoking was automatic dismissal. I don't tell my players that now. I tell them that because they are in the public eye and are seen wherever they go and whatever they do they should feel obligated to set a good example for admiring youngsters.

Probably the peak of excitement in my entire naval career came only weeks before my final discharge. Japan had surrendered and combat carriers were now going to become transports for planes and pilots who were land based in the Pacific. I was just about to report to a overseas assignment when I received deferred orders to the U.S.S. Sable. I had never heard of it. It wasn't listed among the ships of register, and, of all places, I was to report to the Great Lakes Naval Training Station, hardly where you would expect to pick up a combat ship of any kind.

The explanation turned out to be simple. Sable and her sister ship the U.S.S. Wolverine were being used to train young pilots in how to land and take off from a carrier. If a pilot made a mistake or became shy of hitting the deck, he could easily return to the nearby air station and land safely.

When I reported to the executive officer of the Sable, he turned ash white, as if he had seen a ghost. Shocked, he explained that he had been aboard the Franklin and was the last person to speak to Freddie Stalcup and his gun crew before the Japanese kamikaze hit.

The Sable was full of greenhorns like me, getting ready to go overseas and handle patrol duties or whatever tasks remained to bring all the forces home. Of course, having been in the Navy long enough to accumulate sufficient points for separation, I was hoping to be out before my 90-day delay was up. I certainly didn't want to get stuck out in the Pacific for several months.

Time passed all too rapidly until one night shortly before I was to leave. The captain and executive officer having gone ashore, I was the senior officer aboard the ship when a squall came up on Lake Michigan. It was a lulu. The captain had warned me that it might blow up big and ordered three anchors put out. We got the two other anchors out but now the storm was really on when the watch officer called me to the bridge.

A short distance away, an LST (Landing Ship Tank used in amphibious landings) dragging its anchor was heading right at us. There was no way we could get underway; no way, in my mind, to avoid a collision. I could see myself standing before a court martial. I ran back to my quarters to see if the Watch Officer's Guide would tell me what to do. It didn't.

There was nothing we could do but wait. The LST finally blew past our bow. It missed by maybe a hundred feet, but in ships this size that was too close. I was still shaking when the captain came aboard. He agreed that our wait-and-pray solution may not have been good seamanship, but at least there was a ship for the captain to come back to.

It was just after this, thanks to the skipper, and his phone calls to Washington, D.C., that my orders for separation came through. Great Lakes, which was handling separation for anyone living in the Midwest, seemed almost literally in perpetual chaos. The lines were huge, and there seemed to be no end to how long all the red tape would take. As I waited in line with my sheaf of papers it was some comfort to encounter an old friend, the great Notre Dame coach Frank Leahy, also a Naval officer, who was being processed at the same time. We talked so long I was beginning to feel embarrassed about monopolizing him while admirals were waiting to get his attention.

After being separated from the Navy just before Christmas of 1945, I returned to South Bend and to

Central High the Monday after New Year's Day in 1946. Another man had been coaching basketball, but he had been replaced and I picked the team up in mid-season.

Some of the other coaches who had also gone into service were not so fortunate. Their old positions were not made available to them when they returned. I felt this was wrong. A man who had served his country should be given back his same job. It was obvious that although Central was physically the same, and P. D. Pointer was still the principal, my school and the whole South Bend system, for that matter, had changed. And I didn't like the new attitude I found there.

On top of that, we found a change in the city too when we tried to buy back our old home. We had had to let it go when the individual to whom we had leased it didn't pay the rent. We couldn't keep up rent at our service locations and the house in South Bend, too, so we lost it.

Now, less than three years after we had bought it for $6,000, it had a price tag far beyond our reach, and we could not find a satisfactory rental within our means.

All these things, but especially the way some of my friends were being treated about regaining their pre-war positions, made me decide to leave. In the spring of the year several job offers seemed to come to me all at once. There were some opportunities in public relations, another with a fine book publishing company, and some college and good high school coaching offers. Instead I decided to accept a position at Indiana State University in Terre Haute. This seemed a good time to try the college level.

On July 1, 1946, we moved to Indiana State. It was a pretty, little school, with about 2,500 students, although today it has an enrollment of around 15,000. I was athletic director, head basketball and baseball coach and taught those two sports in the physical education department.

After eleven years of high school basketball at Dayton and South Bend, this was a new challenge. My record in high school, while lacking in a state title, was very good. We had won 218 games, lost 42, for a percentage of .839.

It was obvious, however, from the first day that things were going to be different at Indiana State. Almost all the candidates were veterans, many of them married. Most were on the G.I. Bill, but some needed extra work to support their families.

Ironically, a lot of my former South Bend Central players were enrolled as well as some other players from the South Bend school system against whom my Central team had participated prior to World War II. Eddie Pawelski enrolled, but because of an injury, not lack of talent, he was not able to participate.

One of our starting guards, Lennie Rzeszewski, was from Central. When he graduated from high school he was 5 feet 7 inches and perhaps 145. When he turned out for fall practice, he was 6 feet 3 inches and was around 185. He had grown eight inches in the four or so years he was in service.

On that first varsity at Indiana State, I kept fifteen players, fourteen of them freshmen, Bobby Royer, a sophomore guard, was the only starter who was not a veteran. One of the reserves on that first club, Jimmy Powers, later became the basketball coach at Central in South Bend where he developed Mike Warren, who made All-American for us at UCLA.

After winning our conference with an 18 and 7 record that first year, we were invited to the National Association of Intercollegiate Athletics (NAIA) tournament in Kansas City. I refused the invitation. They wouldn't let us bring Clarence Walker, a fine young black reserve from East Chicago, Indiana, along. While he didn't play too much compared to our starters. I felt that the whole team or no team should go.

During the second season at Indiana State, we had another fine club. With a 29 and 7 record we were again invited to the NAIA tournament. This time there was no question about Clarence playing. It was a mighty tough tournament, with Brigham Young headed by Mel

Hutchins, Marshall College with Andy Tonkovitch, Hamline with Harold Haskins and Vern Mikkelsen, and Louisville, all well-schooled basketball teams. We lost to Louisville in the finals. They had an outstanding player in Jack Coleman, who played in the NBA for several years, as well as some other fine players. We might have been an even better team if we hadn't lost one of our expected starters, Freddy Stelow, who had been killed in an auto accident the previous summer.

This year was also unique because it marked the first time I had ever been to Madison Square Garden as either a player or a coach. Piggie Lambert never would take Purdue and was even upset at my taking Indiana State. While I have always preferred to play on a college campus and firmly believe that is where all intercollegiate competition, except for post-season tournament play, should be held, I have always gone to public arenas when necessary or desirable and still do.

After two successful seasons at Indiana State, I began to receive offers to move. One large Big Ten school talked to me indirectly but I didn't appreciate the kind of offer they made. They stated that if I'd stay at Indiana State another year I would be offered the head coaching position. That, to me, meant that the man coaching then was going to be fired and they would like to keep me in the bank to take his position. That didn't set well with me. Apparently, they did not want their present coach, but did not want to pay off his contract.

In a matter of days other offers came my way. My feeling was that it was more in keeping with my philosophy and character to move to a new job on my terms and on my concepts than to be a court appointee in waiting.

10

Things turn out best for those who make the best of the way things turn out.

WITH MY DEPARTURE from South Bend Central, my goal was to move gradually into a coaching position at a major institution. Needless to say, I hoped it would be in the Big Ten where I had played.

It was shortly after our return from Kansas City and our runner-up finish in the NAIA that a number of offers came in. Two, in particular, interested me—the University of Minnesota and the University of California at Los Angeles. I actually favored Minnesota.

Frank McCormick, who was then the athletic director at Minnesota and later became the supervisor of officials in the Pacific Coast Conference, was well acquainted with me from my years as a player at Purdue and in coaching in Indiana. I didn't know how Wilbur Johns of UCLA knew about me until I found out that an old friend, Bob Kelley, formerly a broadcaster of football and basketball games in Indiana and now with the Los Angeles Rams, had first suggested my name to him.

After visiting both Minnesota and UCLA, I had promised to give Frank and Wilbur my answer on an agreed-upon evening. I had decided to take the Minnesota job except for one problem—the retention of Dave McMillan, the man whom I would be replacing, as my assistant. Even though I liked Mr. McMillan, I wanted my own man, Eddie Powell.

Minnesota had to get approval from its board that was meeting this particular day for me to bring Powell and not keep McMillan. As it was set up, McCormick was to call me for my answer at 6:00 P.M. and Johns would call at 7:00. There was a snow storm raging in Minneapolis that day and Frank got snowed in and couldn't get to a phone on time.

I didn't know of the problem so when Mr. Johns called, right on time, I accepted the UCLA job. When McCormick finally reached me about an hour later, he told me everything was "all set."

"It's too late," I told him. "I have already accepted the job at UCLA."

Frank wanted me to call Wilbur back and try to get off the hook, but I refused. I had accepted; UCLA was committed, and had already released the news of my appointment to the press in Los Angeles.

My first impression of UCLA, on my visit, had not been good. I was appalled at the facilities. That was probably the reason I preferred Minnesota. They had a huge fieldhouse while UCLA had a tiny gym that later became known as the "B. O. Barn" when we began to fill it to the ceiling.

While UCLA lacked the major facility, I was led to believe that one was on the drawing boards and was expected within three years. Also the Southern California climate was lovely. I enjoyed playing golf and could do it the year round.

Immediately after accepting the position, I arranged to take a week off from Indiana State and go to Los Angeles to conduct spring basketball practice which was then permitted. On my previous visit I had been all over the campus, visited various administrators and officials, but had not met a one of the basketball players.

When I went up on the floor for the first time in the spring of 1948 and put them through that first practice, I was very disappointed. I felt that my Indiana State team could have named the score against them. I was shattered. Had I known how to abort the agreement in an honorable manner, I would have done so and gone to Minnesota, or if that was impossible, stayed on at Indiana State.

However, that would be contrary to my creed. I don't believe in quitting, so I resolved to work hard, try to develop the talent on hand, and recruit like mad for the next year.

While the talent disturbed me during the five days I worked with them, the discovery that I was not working for the university but rather for the Associated Students really upset me. That meant the student body president was my boss. I had not known, or, didn't understand that when I first looked at the job or I would never have considered it in the first place.

These two factors really contributed toward a harrowing week. It was necessary for me to return to Terre Haute and leave spring practice in the hands of two hold-over assistants from Mr. Johns' staff, Bill Putnam and Don Ashen. But before leaving, I began to delve into just how the junior college system worked in California. Because we had so few junior colleges in the Midwest, I wasn't particularly familiar with them. But I found it hard to believe the junior colleges could help much. Nevertheless I was desperate for help and reviewed some films of jaycee games in which there were some players Putnam and Ashen thought might help.

After the close of school at Indiana State, I moved my family to Los Angeles, realizing that I had a tremendous job ahead to turn things around. By the time regular practice started, the press had already tabbed us to finish last in the old Pacific Coast Conference. The year before, UCLA won 12 and lost 13, and as far as I could determine the three best players—Don Barksdale, Davage Minor, and John Stanich—were gone.

It was like starting from scratch. Almost all of the early practice sessions were devoted to fundamentals, drills, conditioning, and trying to put my philosophy over. Within a few weeks things didn't look quite as dark.

Alan Sawyer, who had not been at practice in the

spring, looked very good at forward. We had obtained Carl Kraushaar from Compton Junior College, and he played center. George Stanich looked like a fine guard, but he, too, had not been out in the spring since he was also a fine high jumper and baseball pitcher. Then there was a little sophomore guard, Eddie Sheldrake, who I knew would do the job. He was cut out of the kind of cloth I like guards made from. And Chuck Clustka was a rugged, hard-driving forward who complemented the fine shooting but poor driving Sawyer.

Ronnie Pearson, who was elected captain; Paul Saunders, another junior college transfer; and the rest developed rapidly, seeming to pick up what I wanted.

We turned things around almost instantly and won the Southern Division title with a 10 and 2 record. However, we lost to Oregon State in Corvallis in the conference playoffs—2 games to 1. In all, we won 22 and lost 7 for the full season—the most wins any UCLA team had ever compiled in history.

We won many of our games that year and in ensuing years more on condition than we did on ability although we rapidly gained more than our share of ability. We were prepared physically to play fast-break, pressure basketball from end line to end line the entire game.

The second year, 1949-50, we were a much better ball club. We had more depth, and the boys had a more thorough understanding of my philosophy of basketball. Again we took the Southern Division, but this time we won the conference title in two close games with Washington State. The Cougars were a very fine club led by Gene Conley, who later played with the Boston Celtics in the NBA and the Boston Braves as a pitcher, and Dave Gambold, who also played in the NBA.

We won that first game in the play-off 60–58, but our playing wasn't all that good. With little time left to play, we had a six to eight point lead, but every time we would go down the floor, Ralph Joeckel, one of our forwards, took a shot he had no business trying. He missed every one of them. Then Washington State would go down and hit and keep closing in, but I couldn't get Joeckel out.

Finally, after another of his wayward shots, Washington State missed, and Ralph got the rebound with the score tied. Ralph dribbled on down the floor to about the center line. Photographs show that he took off with a high arching jump shot just back of the center line in our back court and came down just about the same distance the other side. The ball seemed to go up among the rafters in the old barn, banked off the backboard, and came down through the net just as the gun sounded.

Bedlam broke out when the shot went in. You couldn't see Joeckel in the crowd that poured onto the floor. Finally they carried him off the court and down the winding stairs to the dressing room.

When I finally reached the dressing room, Ralph was at the door. "I sure tried to throw that ball game away, didn't I, coach?"

"You sure did," I responded and resolved then and there to reemphasize to all my players the importance of taking only high percentage shots when protecting a lead.

That shot and the 52–49 win the next night put us in the National Collegiate Athletic Association playoffs for the first time. As we prepared to go east, I thought we had an excellent chance of winning the NCAA. We played Bradley in the first round at Kansas City and had the game won if we just stayed with our style. With less than three minutes to go we had a five or six point lead but fell into a rash of horrible mistakes. It was just a classic example of how to lose a basketball game you had won. I had not properly prepared my players and had no one to blame but myself.

Despite the fact that the first two years had been fairly successful, I was not totally enthralled with UCLA. And it was about this time that various representatives from Purdue were talking to me about going back to West Lafayette. They made a tremendous offer—a lot better financially than the $6,000 I got to come to UCLA. In addition I was to have a perpetual five-year contract with built-in increases that I could renegotiate annually. There were also a number of other amenities, including a family membership in country clubs, a new car every year, a very nice home on campus at a nominal rent, a large insurance policy, and several other so-called fringe benefits.

I agreed to accept the Purdue offer if I could gracefully get out of the final year of my three-year contract at UCLA and arranged for a meeting with Wilbur Johns and Bill Ackerman, then graduate manager of the Associated Students. I fully expected they would decide to release me.

But Wilbur and Bill surprised me. They pointed out that I was the one who had insisted on a three-year contract and felt that I should honor it. They made me feel like a heel for even considering leaving. I was irritated to say the least. Although I understood their position, at the time I felt it was unfair. They offered to amend my contract with an increase in salary for the final year.

"No," I told them. "I signed for three years, and I'll continue for three years."

I was peeved and a bit stubborn. Wilbur later told me he was afraid I would leave for sure when my third year was up, particularly since he saw no hope of a new place to play in the foreseeable future.

But after the third year I decided that it would take a most unusual and unlikely offer to get me to leave, and even then it would be a question. The children had fallen in love with California, and they fought every discussion of moving. I am also one who believes that things always turn out for the best and, even though I could not foresee ever having a team of mine play in our own building on campus, UCLA was a fine school. Furthermore, I could see the caliber of basketball improving every year. This, plus the rapid population growth of the Los Angeles area and the ideal climate, seemed to offer hope for realizing a few of my dreams.

11

*Full many a gem of purest ray serene,
  the deep unfathom'd caves of ocean bear:
Full many a flower is born to blush unseen
  and waste its sweetness on the desert air.**

THOSE WORDS do not apply to Los Angeles. Here you are going to be seen. And there are few places in the world that you are going to be seen as much. I suddenly realized that during my third year in Los Angeles, as I became aware that if we could get a suitable place to play, we would have a plethora of talent available to us as basketball progressed in Southern California.

Here in the third largest city in the nation, we can now point to three dominant college basketball forces in California State at Long Beach, USC, and UCLA. There is no state in the nation, let alone a city, that can present such powers. This in itself creates a natural rivalry that provides a tremendous incentive to coaches and players to succeed. Then when you take in the state and include California, Stanford, Santa Clara, University of the Pacific, and schools like that, it is easy to understand why basketball has boomed.

We must also give due credit to the influx of professional basketball in the state. But I would just as soon not have my boys see a pro game because of the emphasis on individual play, the type of hand checking defense that is illegal for college play, and the bad habits they can pick up. However, I also believe they will

---

* Thomas Gray, *Elegy Written in a Country Churchyard*.

A Gallery of Greatness
High-action photos from the career of
John Wooden

The Wooden family (left to right: Nan, Jim, John, and Nellie) at home in South Bend, Indiana, after John's commissioning as lieutenant (jg) in the United States Navy during World War II.

Joshua Hugh Wooden, John Wooden's father. John credits his father with being the man who has had the greatest influence on his life.

Snapshot shows John Wooden and Nellie Riley during their high school years at Martinsville, Indiana.

At Purdue University, John Wooden, three times an All-American guard, was considered the greatest player in college ranks. Note locker key tied into his left shoe.

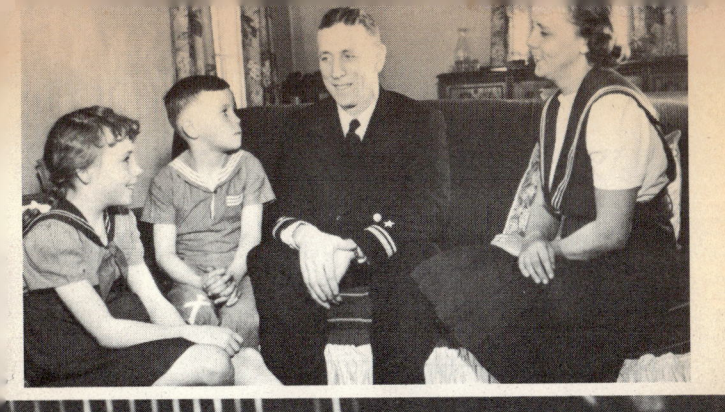

UCLA chancellor and staff meet new coach John Wooden (Far right) shortly after his arrival at Westwood in 1948. Left to right are William Ackerman, head of Associated Students; the late Wilbur Johns, athletic director and retiring basketball coach; Mrs. Rowe Baldwin, ticket manager; the late Dr. Clarence Dykstra, UCLA chancellor; and Mrs. Thelner Hoover, Alumni Association vice-president.

Lewis Alcindor (33), UCLA's three-time All-American, challenges Elvin Hayes of Houston (44) during classic battle won by Houston, 71-69.

With Keith Erickson (left) and Gail Goodrich (second from right), John Wooden receives second successive NCAA championship trophy from the late Bernie Shively. Erickson and Goodrich were co-captains of the 1965 club that defeated Michigan, 91-80.

During dedication of Pauley Pavilion on UCLA campus in December 1965, John Wooden (left) walks down honor guard of his former players and managers with his assistant coach, Jerry Norman.

Family photograph taken November 1970 includes Wooden's wife, children, and grandchildren. Top row, left to right: son-in-law Stan Dennis, daughter Nan Dennis, wife Nellie, son Jim Wooden, daughter-in-law Carleen Wooden; front row, left to right: Caryn Dennis, Cathleen Dennis, Kim Wooden, John holding Michael Wooden, John Wooden (Jim's son), Gregory Wooden, and Christy Dennis.

UCLA's all-winning coach watches the Bruins in play. The results are mirrored in his expressions.

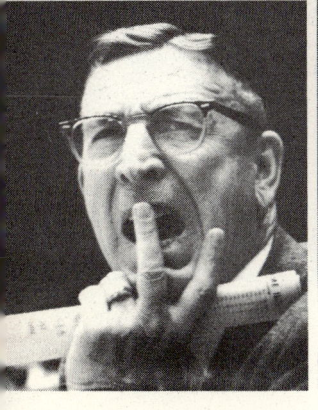

UCLA's NCAA basketball champions following the title victory over Memphis State at St. Louis: Kneeling, from left, student manager Les Freidman, Larry Hollyfield and Larry Farmer. Second row, from left, Casey Corliss and Tommy Curtis. Standing, from left, student manager Ken Jaffe, Vince Carson, Gary Franklin, Keith Wilkes, Ralph Drollinger, Greg Lee, Bill Walton, Bob Webb, Swen Nater, assistant coach Gary Cunningham, Dave Meyers, Pete Trgovich, Andre McCarter and assistant coach Frank Arnold. Second row, far right, coach John Wooden and trainer Ducky Drake.

Wooden explaining a point to senior forward, Larry Farmer.

Coach Wooden and Bill Walton during an informal workout during the 1973 NCAA tournament.

Wooden emphasizing a defensive point.

John Wooden poses before his display in the Basketball Hall of Fame in Springfield, Massachusetts. Wooden is the only man to be in the Hall both as player and as coach.

see many things that can be helpful. But from my point of view the primary value of the pro game has been to develop interest.

The intense competition between the large number of schools in Southern California certainly accounts for the fantastic interest in basketball. Obviously this calls for enormous reservoirs of talent, but happily it is pouring out of the high schools year after year. No one wins without talent, and when you are in the heart of it with an attractive, successful program, you will attract the quality needed to contend nationally. Couple these factors with the construction of several fine playing facilities—the Los Angeles Sports Arena, the Forum, the Long Beach Arena, the Anaheim Arena, and Pauley Pavilion at UCLA—and it is easy to understand the strides made in basketball in the more than twenty years I have been in Los Angeles.

One of the things that truly solidified our program at UCLA was moving into Pauley Pavilion on the UCLA campus in 1966. It seemed to give us a little more incentive. I know I worked just as hard in the years we were playing in everything from the B. O. Barn to the Sports Arena, but I didn't work with the same deep-seated purpose that is inspired by playing in your own facility.

Possibly a frequent comment of mine describes the difference. "Don't mistake activity for achievement."

There is a very fine line between the champion and the runner-up. Six or seven of my teams, in my opinion, had the potential to win the NCAA championships before the 1964 team succeeded. Each might have been good enough to win but the "if" always arose . . . if we had done this or if we had done that, it might have been different. That line between the champion and near champion is something no one can properly define. I can't and I've tried. But I do know that with the first NCAA championship, the dedication of Pauley Pavilion, the appointment of J. D. Morgan as athletic director, the acquisition of two full-time assistants, the transfer to Morgan of schedule-making, and the freedom of not having to prepare a basketball budget, all my efforts became concentrated on one thing—teaching basketball.

It seems to me, too, that the sports climate of Los Angeles contributes to the keenness of competition and the striving toward success. I'm sure that the presence of the Dodgers, the Rams, the Lakers, and our intense cross-town rivalry with USC gives us an incentive to succeed and do well that we might not have in South Bend or a Colorado Springs or an Iowa City. Here we have to hustle to stay up with the success of our peers.

It is essential that we look forward constantly. Looking back could well cause us to stumble and fall.

Still another contributor to the intensity and success of the basketball climate in California is the junior college program. Junior colleges have provided UCLA—and for that matter all the schools in the West—with some excellent talent.

Recently I compiled a rather interesting set of statistics which points out the route by which all of my lettermen came to UCLA. Up through the 1959-60 team 62.1 percent came in from junior colleges. And from 1960 to the present time 56.6 percent picked up some credits from junior college before being admitted to UCLA.

Another factor that makes the California area so fertile for basketball is the overall athletic program. Every sport receives great emphasis, and there is tremendous competition in what many people call minor sports, such as golf, tennis, swimming, soccer, rugby, cross-country, volleyball, water polo, etc.

But I think a key factor is something many states do not have—the classification teams. Most high schools in the area have not only a varsity basketball team but others known as Class B, Class C, and in some cases Class D teams. These teams are formed by boys based on what they call exponents—height, weight, age, etc.—and they play a regular schedule.

Occasionally a young man who is small and slender and playing on the Class B team suddenly blossoms out, grows a few inches, and moves up to the varsity where he will star. Gail Goodrich, who twice made All-American at UCLA and has done amazingly well in the NBA, is one of those little fellows who grew up to become an outstanding player.

There was one factor which I opposed that some believe played an important role in the development of basketball here. It was the so-called "summer leagues" that have since been banned by the NCAA.

Those leagues got completely out of hand. People were "sponsoring" teams made up of California, Stanford, USC, or UCLA players. They might play two or three nights a week around the area. It was way out of bounds and I was very thankful when the NCAA stopped such programs.

Basketball is a great game, and I probably appreciate it as much as the next man, but I've always felt that playing competitively during the summer takes away your college schedule. Furthermore, I do not want my players to miss the value of other things. I want them well rounded.

Now, let's face it: many basketball players are going to play or practice the year around. I've even known some of my kids to play pick-up games when I gave them a day off because I felt they needed a rest. This is fine as long as it is of their own volition.

That merely typifies the intensity of the competitive athlete. Throughout the entire summer, pick-up games are being played practically every day at a dozen places. And there is nothing wrong with that kind of play. The only admonishment I make to my boys is that they police the play, not allow it to get too rough, and try to avoid careless fouls and ball handling because they may carry those bad habits into our games and it could hurt them.

It has always been my contention that controls must be placed on the boys, and controls must govern every facet of the program. Perhaps a better word than control would be organization. Without organization and leadership toward a realistic goal there is no chance of realizing more than a small percentage of your full potential. Every effort should be made, in the proper manner and keeping everything in proper perspective, toward maximum development of both the individual and the group as a whole. Too much emphasis in the off-season can, in my opinion, deprive the players of many other worthwhile activities, and may also cause some to grow stale during your own season.

12

*Success is peace of mind
which is a direct result of
Self-satisfaction in knowing you
did your best to become the
Best you are capable of becoming.*

DEFINITIONS of success vary. And everyone has a different degree of acceptance of success. My own quest for an acceptable definition began when I was in Martinsville High School. One of our teachers, Lawrence Schidler, gave the class an assignment—to define success. He had tried to point out to us that success didn't necessarily mean the accumulation of material possessions or a position of power or prestige.

That started me thinking about just what a proper definition of success would be for John Wooden. Through my years in high school and college I thought about it many times but never really had the time to delve into it deeply. While I was at South Bend Central, in the middle to late '30s, I again became concerned over what success really was or should be.

Perhaps it was a selfish concern. I don't know. But a part of my concern was due to the fact that many parents judged teachers by the marks their children received in class. If the grades were good, the teacher was good, and if the grades were poor, it was the teacher's fault.

I began to try to develop a paper that would help my students to understand how to judge success. I had seen various ladders of success so I began using blocks with key words followed by an expanded definition.

Over the next few years, and after hundreds of hours

of effort, I developed what is now known as John Wooden's Pyramid of Success. My definition is at the top of the pyramid. Only one person can judge it—you. You can fool everyone else, but in the final analysis only you know whether you goofed off or not. You know if you took the shortcut, the easy way out, or cheated. No one else does. I know that I look back with regret on some things that seemed to be success to others.

Over the years, I have given out literally thousands of copies of the pyramid. Once a year on my Los Angeles television show, we offer the pyramid to those who write and ask for it. Each year we send out several thousand. A couple of years ago, Leonard Le Sourd wrote an article about it in *Guideposts* magazine and mentioned that I would send a copy to all who wrote for it. This got completely out of hand. After mailing out several thousand, we started bundling up the requests and sending them to *Guideposts* for distribution. That article brought requests for some fifteen thousand.

Today at the beginning of every season and of all my summer camps, the pyramid is discussed in detail and each person is given a copy of it. I firmly believe it can be a base for anyone to build upon.

No building is better than its structural foundation, and no man is better than his mental foundation. Therefore, my original cornerstones are still the same —*industriousness* and *enthusiasm*. There is no substitute for work. And to really work hard at something you must enjoy it. If you're not enthusiastic, you can't work up to your maximum ability.

One of the late Grantland Rice's writings epitomizes my feelings on the role industriousness plays in success, especially athletic success.

> You wonder how they do it and you look to
> see the knack,
> You watch the foot in action, or the
> shoulder, or the back,

> But when you spot the answer where the
> higher glamours lurk,
> You'll find in moving higher up the
> laurel covered spire,
> That the most of it is practice and the
> rest of it is work.*

Then three attributes that I placed in the base between the cornerstones are *friendship, cooperation,* and *loyalty.* They are all similar and help illustrate that it takes united effort to tie in the cornerstones.

The anchor blocks of the second tier of the pyramid are *self-control* and *intentness.* If you lose self-control everything will fall. You cannot function physically or mentally or in any other way unless your emotions are under control. That's why I prefer my team to maintain a constant, slightly increasing level of achievement rather than hitting a number of peaks. I believe that there is a corresponding valley for every peak, just as there is a disappointment for every joy. The important thing is that we recognize the good things and not get lost in self-pity over misfortunes.

For an athlete to function properly he must be intent. There has to be a definite purpose and goal if you are to progress. If you are not intent about what you are doing, you aren't able to resist the temptation to do something else that might be more fun at the moment.

Alertness and *initiative* are within the second tier. You've got to be constantly alive and alert and looking for ways to improve. This is especially true in basketball. You must be alert to take advantage of an opponent's error or weakness. Coupled with this must be the individual initiative to act alone. You must have the courage to make decisions.

Now at the heart of the pyramid is *condition.* I stress this point with my players. I don't mean physical condition only. You cannot attain and maintain physical condition only. You cannot attain and maintain physi-

---
* Grantland Rice, "How to Be a Champion."

cal condition unless you are morally and mentally conditioned. And it is impossible to be in moral condition unless you are spiritually conditioned. I tell my players that our team condition depends on two factors—how hard they work on the floor during practice and how well they behave between practices. You can neither attain nor maintain proper condition without working at both.

At the very center—the heart of the structure—is *skill*. Skill, as it pertains to basketball, is the knowledge and the ability to quickly and properly execute the fundamentals. Being able to do them is not enough. They must be done quickly. And being able to do them quickly isn't enough either. They must be done quickly and precisely at the right time. You must learn to react properly, almost instinctively.

Team spirit is also an important block in the heart of the structure. This is an eagerness to sacrifice personal glory for the welfare of the group as a whole. It's togetherness and consideration for others. If players are not considerate of one another, there is no way we can have the proper team play that is needed. It is not necessary for everyone to particularly like each other to play well together, but they must respect each other and subordinate selfishness to the welfare of the team. The team must come first.

Poise and *confidence* will come from condition, skill, and team spirit. To have poise and be truly confident you must be in condition, know you are fundamentally sound, and possess the proper team attitude. You must be prepared and know that you are prepared.

Near the pinnacle must be *competitive greatness*. And this cannot be attained without poise and confidence. Every block is built upon the other. One will not succeed without the other, and when all are in place, you are on the road toward success. If one crumbles, it may lead to the breakdown of all.

Grantland Rice's writing again illustrates well the role of competitive greatness in the game of life or sport in his marvelous poem, "The Great Competitor":

> Beyond the winning and the goal, beyond the
> glory and the fame,
> He feels the flame within his soul, born of
> the spirit of the game,
> And where the barriers may wait, built up
> by the opposing Gods,
> He finds a thrill in bucking fate and riding down the endless odds.
> Where others wither in the fire or fall below some raw mishap,
> Where others lag behind or tire and break
> beneath the handicap,
> He finds a new and deeper thrill to take him
> on the uphill spin,
> Because the test is greater still, and something he can revel in.

This pyramid is tied together with a number of other qualities that are essential to the ultimate definition of success. You tie them together with *ambition,* which if properly focused, can be a tremendous asset, but if it is out of focus, it can be a detriment. You must be *adaptable* to work with others and to meet the challenge of different situations. And you must display *resourcefulness* because in almost every situation good judgment is necessary.

Fight gives you the ability to do it and not be afraid of a tough battle. *Faith* must walk beside *fight* because it is essential that you believe in your objective, and you can't have faith without prayer. *Patience* must be strong because the road will be rough at times and you should not expect too much too soon. Then come *reliability, integrity, honesty,* and *sincerity.*

All of these tie the blocks together into a solid structure. When all these factors are united, you can build toward a success that is based on your own personal set of goals, not those of someone else.

Some skeptics, and there have been a few of my players among them, question whether the pyramid really accomplishes anything. I can't answer that. Each person has to answer that for himself. All I know is that I receive request after request from all types of organizations to speak about my pyramid. I do believe it can help everyone to some degree, and certainly can't hurt anyone.

A number of people have suggested that I copyright the pyramid and sell it, but I have refused. If in some small way this chart will help others, then that is enough for me. It was not created to be sold but to be used as a teaching tool, and it has been used just as much in the classroom as on the court.

There have been many players, especially after graduation, who come back and ask for a few copies.

"Coach," they'll tell me, "it's been a great benefit to me."

The youngsters who attend my basketball schools in the summer are always eager to receive copies of the pyramid, and some of them even ask for extra copies for younger brothers and sisters. I make it a policy to personally autograph each copy, and this seems to make a great impression on the youngsters.

Even my UCLA players are youngsters until they get out and are on their own. Then they begin to understand and appreciate what we are trying to instill through the pyramid. Steve Patterson, our fine center on that power line with Curtis Rowe and Sidney Wicks, recently came by after his first year in the NBA to tell me that now he realizes what I was driving at.

Patterson is not unusual. I feel that similar circumstances take place every year with every coach and with every player. I am highly flattered by a comment made by Bart Starr, the famous Green Bay Packer quarterback, in his book *A Perspective on Victory* (Follett Publishing Co., 1972).

"To continue to win is the mark of a champion. Of a winner. I think John Wooden at UCLA is a good example of that.

"What he's done year in and year out over the past decade is fabulous. He continues to win because he has something going for those young men that will help sustain them for the rest of their lives. His philosophy is very much the same as Coach Vince Lombardi's was. Coach Wooden equates basketball to the game of life. He says you have to be unselfish, that you have to play for the good of the team, that you have to be disciplined and do what he wants you to do as a team, that he will tolerate no individuality within that team. He wants you to play as a unit. This is really what you end up doing in life because sooner or later you end up on a team."

That's what you try to get across, but you have to constantly remind yourself that the Pattersons and the Wickses are young.

Sidney Wicks has lectured at some of the summer basketball schools for me. He has a marvelous rapport with kids, especially the little ones. Here's this huge man, towering over them by several feet, talking to them about the basics of the pyramid, and they are enthralled.

"You suddenly realize," Sidney tells them, "that all those things Coach Wooden harps on all the time are true. So take it from me, pay attention, do it Coach Wooden's way. It's right."

Sidney's words pretty well typify most of the young men who leave me. We have given them a foundation; now it is up to them to improve the structure.

13

*Remember this your lifetime through—
Tomorrow, there will be more to do . . .
And failure waits for all who stay
With some success made yesterday . . .
Tomorrow, you must try once more
And even harder than before.*

IT IS MOST difficult, in my mind, to separate any success, whether it be in your profession, your family, or as in my case, in basketball, from religion.

In my profession, I must be deeply concerned with God's belief in me and be truly interested in the welfare of my fellow-man. No coach should be trusted with the tremendous responsibility of handling young men under the great mental, emotional, and physical strain to which they are subjected unless he is spiritually strong. If he does possess this inner strength, it is only because he has faith and truly loves his fellow-man. This was the belief of Amos Alonzo Stagg, who also felt the obligations, opportunities, and responsibilities in coaching are manifold. The coach who is committed to the Christlike life will be helping youngsters under his supervision to develop wholesome disciplines of body, mind, and spirit that will build character worthy of his Master's calling. He must set the proper example by work and by deed. It is not easy.

It is my belief that in one way or another we are all seeking success. And success is peace of mind, a direct result of self-satisfaction in knowing that you did your best to become the best that you are capable of becoming, and not just in a physical way. "Seek ye first His Kingdom and His righteousness and all these things will be yours as well."

I try to get this idea across to my players and know that I must practice what I preach if it is to be effective. There are many things that are essential to arriving at true peace of mind, and one of the most important is faith which cannot be acquired without prayer.

Webster partially defines faith as an unquestioning belief in God with complete trust, confidence, and reliance. Faith is not just waiting, hoping, and wanting things to happen. Rather it is working hard to make things happen and realizing that there are no failures—just disappointments—when you have done your best. As someone once said, "If you do your best, angels can do no better."

I try to convince my players that they can never be truly successful or attain peace of mind unless they have the self-satisfaction of knowing they have done their best. Although I want them to work to win, I try to convince them they have always won when they have done their best.

It isn't what you do, but how you do it. No system is any good if the players are not well grounded in fundamentals. Team play comes from integrating individuals who have mastered the fundamentals into a smooth working unit. Confidence comes from being prepared.

And approval is a great motivator. I try to follow any criticism, whenever possible, with a pat on the back, realizing that I cannot antagonize and influence at the same time. We attempt always to give public credit and acclaim to our play-makers, our defensive men, and those whose role doesn't leap out of the statistical chart.

Playing basketball for UCLA is a privilege, not a right, and every player should work harmoniously with his teammates for the common good of all.

At the same time it should be recognized that basketball is not the ultimate. It is of small importance in comparison to the total life we live. There is only one kind of a life that truly wins, and that is the one that places faith in the hands of the Savior. Until that is done, we are on an aimless course that runs in circles and goes nowhere. Material possessions, winning scores, and great reputations are meaningless in the eyes of the Lord, because He knows what we really are and that is all that matters.

> To have your name inscribed up there is
>   greater yet by far,
> Than all the halls of fame down here and
>   every man-made star.
> This crowd on earth, they soon forget the
>   heroes of the past,
> They cheer like mad until you fall and that's
>   how long you last.
> I tell you, friend, I would not trade my name
>   however small,
> If written there beyond the stars in that
>   celestial hall
> For any famous name on earth or glory that
>   they share,
> I'd rather be an unknown here and have my
>   name up there.*

Today we hear a lot of criticism of our young people, but one thing we cannot fault them on is their growing interest in religion. My own interest in the Lord and especially in reading the Bible comes directly from my father. I read from the Bible every day, sometimes more than once.

There's a story about the small brown New Testament that is on my desk. For the past several years, I have worked at a summer basketball school at Campbell College, a small school in Buie's Creek, North Carolina. One year I went east and discovered that I had left my Bible at home. I got this small one in a book store, and since it is handy to refer to, I have kept it on my desk ever since. Once in a while one of my new players will pick it up when he comes in and finds me busy on the phone. Some of them used to be startled

---

* "God's Hall of Fame," source unknown.

when they opened it, but not any more. Frequently, many of them read a bit while I complete my call.

In addition to the New Testament, I get a great deal of help from reading the *Daily Word* and *The Upper Room*. I also carry a letter in my wallet entitled "Where to look in the Bible." It points out specific references that will be of help in time of need: "When desiring Inward Peace . . . When things look blue . . . When Tempted to do Wrong," etc.

For many years I have been a deacon of the First Christian Church in Santa Monica. I remember the first Sunday, shortly after we moved to Los Angeles, that we went to services with the children. Much to my amazement, as we went up the walk to the entry, I read the minister's name on the bulletin board. It was Wales E. Smith. Now, I had known a Wales Smith when he was a classmate of mine at Martinsville High, but as far as I knew, he was a pastor in Kokomo, Indiana. However, when the minister walked out for the service, it was our Wales Smith. What a happy surprise! He continued to be our pastor until his recent retirement.

It seems to me that man has a great need to communicate with the Lord. For years now, I have carried a little cross in my pocket. Few people, except my immediate family, are aware of it at all. It is clutched in my hand during all of our games and whenever I anticipate tension. A friend, my minister at the First Christian Church in South Bend, the late Rev. Frank E. Davidson, gave it to me just before I went into the navy in 1943, and I've carried it in my pocket ever since.

Frank E. Davidson was a most unique man. He directed the Forum Club for men which replaced regular Sunday school class. Ultimately, it involved people of all faiths—Methodist, Presbyterian, Jewish, Catholic— and became rather famous. It was just what its name implied, a forum on religion and life. One Sunday, I was to receive a button for attending 52 consecutive weeks. This was in the heart of the Indiana State basketball playoffs and two local schools—Central and Washington—were to meet for the regional championship on the previous night.

At the presentation the next morning, Dr. Davidson told a little story: "I sat there last night waiting for the game, aware that Coach Wooden was to receive his '52 button' today. As the teams went into the huddles before the tip, I looked at Coach John How, a Catholic, a member of our club, and saw his players crossing themselves in prayer. I knew John Wooden was quietly saying a little prayer, and I just couldn't help but think, 'Now isn't the Lord in a hell of a spot.' " Then he congratulated me on winning the game, and being perfect in attendance.

Perhaps there isn't an hour of a waking day that I don't think of Frank Davidson. Every time I reach in my pocket for my pocketknife or comb, my fingers touch the cross he gave me. I've worn it down quite a bit from clenching it in my left hand during games. I feel it definitely enables me to better control my emotions.

When I've got a firm grip on it, I'm reminded to take care. This is especially true when it comes to my running comments during the game. I've been known to chide an official to watch "that butcher," meaning some tough, hard-nosed kid pushing one of my players around. I made that remark one time to Ken Stanley, one of USC's fine players and a boy I admired so much for his tough style. Ken became highly incensed over that remark, and rightly so. I don't think I do that quite as much any more, and this little cross is partly responsible.

Another cherished friend who would prefer to remain anonymous sent me the following lines a few years ago. I feel they best describe my association with the little cross.

> I carry a cross in my pocket,
> A simple reminder to me of the fact
>   that I am a Christian wherever I may be;
> This little cross is not magic, nor is it

a good luck charm,
It isn't meant to protect me from every
   physical harm;
It's not for identification for all the
   world to see,
It's simply an understanding between
   my Savior and me;
When I put my hand in my pocket to bring
   out a coin or a key,
The cross is there to remind me of the
   price He paid for me;
It reminds me, too, to be thankful for my
   blessings day by day, and to strive
   to serve Him better in all that I do
   and say;
It is also a daily reminder of the peace
   and comfort I share with all who know
   my Master and give themselves to His care;
So I carry a cross in my pocket reminding
   me, no one but me, that Jesus Christ is
   the Lord of my life if only I will let
   Him be.

We who coach have great influence on the lives of all the young men who come under our supervision, and the lives we lead will play an important role in their future. It is essential that we regard this as a sacred trust and set the example that we know is right. We must try to prevent the pressures for winning scores from causing us to swerve from moral principles.

That's why in the years since I was given this small cross that I grasp it tightly in my hand during games to seek support in maintaining my composure and my emotions no matter how heated the game may be. If I am able to control myself, perhaps it will help my boys to control their emotions and play up to their true potential. I know that I have faltered at times, but I also know that it has been most helpful at times.

Often I tell coaches assembled at clinics throughout

the world that I am somewhat like the unknown fellow who said:

> I am not what I ought to be,
> not what I want to be,
> not what I am going to be,
> But thankful that I am not what I used to be.

14

*Be a gentleman at all times.
Never criticize, nag, or razz a teammate.
Be a team player always.
Never be selfish, jealous, envious, or
 egotistical.
Earn the right to be proud and confident.
Never expect favors, alibi or make excuses.
Never lose faith or patience.
Courtesy and politeness are a small price
 to pay for the good will and affection of
 others.
Acquire peace of mind by becoming the best
 that you are capable of becoming.**

MY LIFE has been wrapped around the family structure and the church from my earliest memory. My personal family life—with my wife, my children and my grandchildren—is merely an extension of a life-style formed in my boyhood with my mother, father, and brothers.

As long as I can remember, Sunday was set aside for the family and for the church. As a boy, this pattern was established. We would go to services, then either go home for dinner with the family and friends, or go to a friend's home for the dinner.

When Nellie and I were married, our life seemed to fall into a similar pattern. And when we moved to South Bend our own family Sunday ritual became firmly established. After Sunday school and the worship service, we would go some place to eat with the Kindys or some other friends and occasionally we drove to Benton Harbor, Michigan, to be with the Perigo family.

Walt Kindy came to Central High the same year I did and became my assistant in basketball and ultimately my assistant in all other capacities—tennis, baseball, comptroller, and athletic director. And Bill Perigo, who later coached basketball at the University of Michigan, became a close friend through our playing pro basketball together with Kautsky's. When we moved

---
* From Wooden's set of normal expectations.

to South Bend, Bill was coaching at Benton Harbor, Michigan, not far across the Indiana line.

When we moved to Los Angeles our life followed a similar style except for being in a new city and finding new friends. Then as the years passed, our daughter, Nan, and our son, Jim, grew up, became very involved with life, UCLA, and then married.

Nancy Ann became Mrs. Stanley Dennis and now has three lovely daughters, Christy Ann, Caryn Audrey, and Cathleen Amy. James Hugh, who was named after my father, met Carleen Garcia from Hawaii after he was discharged from the Marine Corps. Now they have three handsome sons—Gregory James, John Todd, and Michael Hugh—and Kim Louise, our fourth lovely granddaughter, to share our love. Our lives have truly been enriched by our children and grandchildren.

Our family makes for quite a handful for dinner after Sunday services. It's also a problem for all of us to get together. Nan lives in Reseda, quite some distance out in the San Fernando Valley, and Jimmy now lives in Irvine, near the southern end of Orange County.

We almost always are with our children on Sunday afternoons unless we are out of the city. I recall so well the Sunday after we won the 1970 NCAA title against Jacksonville at the University of Maryland. All the family had come to the airport to meet us, and we had gone home to leave our things, freshen up a bit, and go to dinner with Nan and Stan and the girls. We were taking the family to Lawry's Prime Rib, our favorite restaurant.

We were about to go out the door when the phone rang. When I answered, the operator said "Long distance calling." I waited and waited and waited. It seemed a long while. The grandchildren were impatient to go, Nellie was waving at me, and Cathleen was pulling me by the arm.

"Operator," I said as she came back on the line for a second, "I'm ready to take my family out to dinner. They are all waiting. If this isn't something important, I'm just going to have to leave. I can't wait any longer."

"Sir," she said, "the President of the United States is calling."

"In that case, I'll wait," I stammered, covering the phone with my hand and trying to explain to the children. Of course, when I told them President Nixon was calling, they really were excited.

The president explained that he had tried to call me in College Park the night we won only to learn that we had left for home right after the game. He congratulated us on our victory, said how much he enjoyed watching it and was very gracious and nice.

"Mr. President," I told him, "I have three of my granddaughters here. It would be a tremendous thrill if they could talk to the President of the United States." He talked and visited with each one of them.

One of the greatest compliments I believe I have ever received came from Christy, my oldest granddaughter and first grandchild. When she was in the third grade, one of her assignments was to write a paper entitled, "The Person I Admire Most." She wrote,

> The person I admire most is my grandfather. His name is John Robert Wooden. He is very fond of sports and coaches basketball. I am fond of his great skills in both coaching and playing. He also taught English, and I admire the way he can write rhymes. I am also very fond of the way he handles children, as he does with my little sisters and cousins. I admire all his talents and wish I could have some of them.
>
> Christy, Oct. 22, 1968

Now on most Sundays we go to lunch with various friends from the First Christian Church in Santa Monica. More often than not we eat at Jerry's, a little restaurant on Santa Monica Boulevard where everyone knows everybody else by his first name. Nellie insists that the real reason I like to go there is because they always save me a piece of fresh apricot pie. It's almost as good as our mothers used to make back in Indiana.

After lunch with our friends, we usually hurry home, change our clothes, and drive over to see the children. Now that they live so far apart, it is an increasing problem for all of us to get together as much as we would like.

Occasionally Nellie and I like to get away alone. One of the places we enjoy so much is Welcome Inn, a Lawrence Welk enterprise located near Escondido in Southern California. They have a tricky little 18-hole par-3 golf course, a Jacuzzi pool in which I like to relax several times a day, a beautiful swimming pool, a fine restaurant, and the setting is very peaceful and restful.

I can work the crossword puzzle in the morning after breakfast, and then catch up on my reading. I don't know how many times I've read and reread the Zane Grey series, *Magnificent Obsession* and *The Robe* by Lloyd Douglas, and many books of poems. The late Paul Wellman, whose historical novels are so well done, is one of my choice authors, not only because he was a friend for most of the years we have been at UCLA, but also because his work is so appealing to me.

It was during one of these times of relaxation some years back that I made the decision to give up smoking for good. I had been a cigarette smoker since my days in the service in the Second World War. While I was never a heavy smoker, I did smoke regularly except that each year I would quit on October 14, my birthday, and not smoke again until basketball season was over.

Now my boys can't point to me as being a smoker, even though I didn't smoke during the season and never in front of them. It's pretty hard to expect a boy not to do something that he knows you do. I try to live the life I want them to follow.

15

> *It is amazing how much can be accomplished if no one cares who gets the credit.*

UNSELFISHNESS is a trait I always insist upon. Every basketball team is a unit, and I don't separate them as to starters and subs. Every man plays a role, including the coach, the assistants, the trainer and the managers.

My managers are part of our team. They are not the team's servants. Rather, they work for the team, and the team has to work for them. One of my demand rules has to do with the way we leave our dressing room, either at Pauley Pavilion or on the road. Many building custodians across the country will tell you that UCLA leaves the shower and dressing room the cleanest of any team. We pick up all the tape, never throw soap on the shower floor for someone to slip on, make sure all showers are turned off, and all towels are accounted for. The towels are always deposited in a receptacle if there is one or stacked neatly near the door.

It seems to me that this is everyone's responsibility—not just the manager's. Furthermore, I believe it is a form of discipline that should be a way of life, not to please some building custodian, but as an expression of courtesy and politeness that each of us owes to his fellow-man. These little things establish a spirit of togetherness and consideration and help unite the team into a solid unit.

In my early years as a coach, I ran a pretty taut ship. Every detail was spelled out from the cut of the player's hair to the style of dress for games. I still probably have a tighter rein on my players than most coaches, but it's much looser than before. There is no way I can keep a constant eye on them all of the time, and I'm not going to sit up all night in some hotel lobby to make sure they don't sneak out. Rather, I try to develop a personal concern among them that my requirements are dictated only for their good and ultimate success.

I'm still very strict about being on time for practice and team meals. But I have relaxed my rules on dress by no longer insisting that the team wear jackets, dress shirts, and ties in public. Sport shirts are okay, but I still prefer that a tie be worn with a dress shirt. If we are having a team meal in a private dining room, I will allow them to dress casually, but if we are in a public dining room, I want them to look nice, both for themselves and for the university. Politeness, cleanliness, and neatness are characteristics that should be expected, not demanded.

Over the years I have become convinced that every detail is important and that success usually accompanies attention to little details. It is this, in my judgment, that makes for the difference between champion and near champion.

One of the little things I watch closely is a player's socks. No basketball player is better than his feet. If they hurt, if his shoes don't fit, or if he has blisters, he can't play the game. It is amazing how few players know how to put on a pair of socks properly. I don't want blisters, so each year I give in minute detail a step-by-step demonstration as to precisely how I want them to put on their socks—every time. Believe it or not, there's an art to doing it right, and it makes a big difference in the way a player's feet stand the pounding of practice and the game. Wrinkles which cause blisters can be eliminated by just a little attention.

Along this same line, I attach great importance to the shoes our players wear and how they fit. When most of them come to us, they are wearing shoes a size to a size and a half too large. This seems to be a holdover from childhood, but our players' feet aren't going to grow much. If they do, we'll resize them with new shoes. I want the toe of the foot to be exactly at the end of the shoe when they are standing up so that when they make a quick stop, the foot won't slide.

For most of my coaching life, my teams have worn Converse shoes. I wore them in high school and at Purdue. In all probability I was among the last of the coaches to switch from black, high-top Converse to white high-tops. And I'm sure that I was among the last to go to low-cuts for those players who wanted to wear them. Then a few years ago several players said they would like to try another make of shoe. Finally, I agreed to try them, and said that if the majority of the team voted to wear them, we would change. Since then my players have almost unanimously favored the shoe we now wear. This could change any year, however, as I let the majority decide. A little-known fact is that some players, usually guards, are very hard on shoes and may go through a half-dozen pair a year.

Our uniforms are all alike, even at practice. That's part of my discipline. I don't want one guy practicing in a high school shirt, another wearing a castoff football jersey, another in green shorts, and someone else in yellow. It is important to me that the team be dressed alike, with shirttails in and socks pulled up.

I have been using the same type and make of practice shirt and pant since the 1930s, and our game uniforms and warm-up suits are made to measure for each boy. I design them and have each player measured for fit. When the uniforms arrive, we have an inspection to be sure they fit. If they are not just right, they go back for revision. The players should feel proud of their appearance and be comfortable for both practice and games.

It's the little details that are vital. Little things make big things happen, and that's what I try to get across to my players.

My talks with the players usually take place right on

the floor during practice. I'm not a believer in meetings or so-called chalk talks or blackboard drills. I believe in learning by repetition to the point that everything becomes automatic. Only very rarely do I stop group action to correct one player, as I prefer to explain to an individual his specific mistakes. I do not believe in having several players stand idly by while I am talking to one. But if I do call the team together in a meeting, it is usually for the purpose of making a major change in our offense or defense or to correct a first-time mistake that I want all to be aware of. I feel that the basics can best be presented at one session. However, it is only common sense not to digress and take thirty minutes to explain what should take only five or ten.

We don't have a playbook at UCLA. Years ago, I issued a rather expansive playbook but I became convinced the players didn't pay much attention to it so it was abandoned. Now when I give them a sheet or two of information once in a while, I think they pay more attention to it. But basically, I try to get my "notebook" across verbally every day, bit by bit.

The best teacher is repetition, day after day, throughout the season. I never give my teams any kind of a written test. After all, they don't have time in a game to sit down and write something. It must be instant recognition and instant reaction.

I still keep personal notebooks that I update after every game or at the end of the season. One is a statistical record of what we have done. Another is a coaching book of drills and practices. I can go back twenty-four years and tell you what we did at 3:30 P.M. on a given afternoon. The third book is really a zipper binder that I use when I am at clinics. It's a collection of diverse materials from lectures to play diagrams to poetry to speeches on various aspects of the game.

Then there are the notes to myself. These are cautions to be alert to certain things. For example, "Be more strict about being on the floor at 3:15 P.M." . . . "Organize my time-outs better" . . . "In three-man drills have the shooter take the shot from outside the lane and use the backboard" . . . "Be ready for all types of zone defenses" . . . "Emphasize team play" . . . "Prevent internal problems of any kind early."

Many of these little admonitions originate each day in planning practice. My assistant and I spend about two hours every morning closeted away planning a practice that may not last that long. Every entry is made on a white 3 x 5 card that I carry in my pocket. As things develop during practice that I want to note, I write them on this card. Then I transfer the schedule and my comments into my notebook.

One of my constant reminders is, "End practice on a happy note." I want the boys to want to come out to practice, and I want them to get a certain amount of pleasure out of basketball. It's a game. It should be fun. So I always try to counterbalance any criticism in practice with a bit of praise. I want my players to feel that the worst punishment I can give them is to deny them the privilege of practicing. If they do not want to practice, I do not want them there.

16

If you keep too busy learning the tricks of the trade, you may never learn the trade.

MANY DIFFERENT people influence a man's life. My father had a tremendous influence on mine. So did Glenn Curtis, my high school coach, and Piggie Lambert of Purdue. Some of my dedication to organization comes from Frank Leahy, the former Notre Dame football coach. I often went to his practices and observed how he broke them up into periods. Then I would go home and analyze why he did things certain ways. As a player, I realized there was a great deal of time wasted. Leahy's concepts reinforced my ideas and helped in the ultimate development of what I do now.

Another man who has influenced me by observation rather than association is Walter Alston, the manager of the Los Angeles Dodgers. He has been called the "Quiet Man," but I believe a better description is the "Patient Man." While I am not intimately acquainted with Walter Alston, I can spot his tremendous virtues merely by watching him during a game.

I once heard Al Campanis, the Dodgers' general manager, describe Alston's ability to handle players. "Alston is like a man handling a dove. If you squeeze it too tightly, you'll smother or kill it. If you hold it too loose, it'll fly away."

That's the way I try to work with players. They are just like doves. Some need to be held a little tighter or they'll get out of your control. Others don't need to be held as tightly in order to get the best out of them. There is no standard that will work for all, but above all, a coach must be patient.

As a player, I realized that the good Lord had blessed me with tremendous quickness and a driving desire to be the best conditioned player in basketball. It took me quite a while to realize that the great majority of players would not pay the price of conditioning unless they were driven. Later on I came to see that you could make them work if you kept after them and repeated things time and again. But they can never be forced to do anything by brute strength. It was like one of our old mules—you could hitch him to the wagon or the plow, but you could not make him go. I continually tell my teams that the last law of learning—repetition—is the most important.

In game play it has always been my philosophy that patience will win out. By that, I mean patience to follow our game plan. If we do believe in it, we will wear the opposition down and will get to them. If we break away from our style, however, and play their style, we're in trouble. And if we let our emotions command the game rather than our reason, we will not function effectively.

I constantly caution our teams: "Play your game, just play your game. Eventually, if you play your game, stick to your style, class will tell in the end." This does not mean that we will always outscore our opponent, but does insure that we will not beat ourselves.

It seems to me that more games are lost than are won. That's why scouts have little difficulty writing a report on UCLA. We seldom change our attack—we seldom introduce new patterns—but we try never to lock ourselves into doing the same thing in the same situation. We are not too concerned about opponents knowing what we do as long as they don't know when.

An important ingredient of patience is perseverance. I try to instill in our players the desire to do everything correctly—not to give up on something but to persevere until it is mastered.

Over the years, I have been asked repeatedly which of my UCLA players I would rate as the best. I have never answered that question. But I will say that I have never had any more successful players—by my definition—than Conrad Burke or Doug McIntosh. It wasn't so much because of what they did but how they did it. They weren't especially gifted physically, and they weren't particularly fast or maneuverable. But by perseverance and dedicated hard work they learned their assignments minutely and made few mistakes.

Burke was a starter for two and a half years and McIntosh for two years, although as freshmen, neither one had looked as if he ever would be a starter or even earn a letter. Yet Burke made the starting five midway through his sophomore season in 1956. McIntosh came in to play that great game in the NCAA finals in place of Fred Slaughter in 1964 and started the next two seasons. Neither did it with any tricks, fancy stuff, or brilliant talent. Patience, perseverance, and desire made them major contributors. They truly made the most of the ability they possessed. Who can do more?

It is because of the Burkes and the McIntoshes that I exercise strong patience before I make the ultimate selection of a starting team. Many players have begged me to start, but their practice performance didn't merit it. Only Eddie Powell ever got me to compromise and that's one I'll never understand.

There are only five starting positions. I feel two, or maybe, three others can support them. Therefore, it is important that I not predetermine those starters without giving every man on the squad the opportunity to work his way into that unit.

The older and more experienced men usually start out running on the first five when practice begins. They earned that right the year before even though I may have strong feelings that a younger man, perhaps a sophomore or a junior who came on strong toward the end of the previous season, may be the best. I experiment and try to give them all an equal opportunity.

During preseason practice I work different combinations and try different units on both offense and defense so as to obtain a full evaluation of all players. And then I try to reach a decision before our first game, or definitely by mid-December.

The starting unit is selected when I have determined their combined strength from the composite results from our set offense, our fast-break offense, our set defense, our pressing defense, and best use of first replacements. It is the sum total of the entire unit that counts, not the total of any one part. I must be patient first in my evaluation and then in my selection.

This is a very emotional time both for the players and for me. To them particularly, it is a highly charged period in their lives. Every player believes he is capable of starting. I wouldn't want them if they thought otherwise. Yet only five will start, seven to eight will see considerable playing time, and the rest are charged with keeping our system going to produce the highest level of competition.

While these are trying times for everyone's emotions, I have a firm policy never to charge up my team on an emotional level. For every artificial peak you may create there is a valley, and I don't like valleys. Games can be lost in valleys. The ideal is an ever-mounting graph line that peaks with your final performance. There will be difficulty and adversity to overcome, but that is necessary to become stronger.

Other coaches believe in charging a team up. I never have and never will. I seek a calm assurance in our dressing room, a calm assurance warming up on the floor, and a calm assurance in my final remarks before going out to play. But once that game starts, it's a different matter. I never try to get a Walt Hazzard emotionally high, for example, before the tip. However, once we're underway, I will. I might yell something to him as he goes by, or call some substitute's name to come sit beside me as Hazzard is going by. I'll do anything that might work to shake loose a lethargic situation.

I am citing Walt Hazzard only as a name, not as an individual. Walter didn't have to be charged up very much once he assimilated our philosophy. Like so many other of my players, Walter always came to play.

There is a fine line between spirit and temperament. I want spirit and deride temperament. Keith Erickson, probably one of the greatest defensive players I've ever coached, rode that line like a silver bullet. Few have balanced it like Keith did.

Keith was the kind of young man who loved to test me to see how far he could go. He was mischievous but not mean. Not bad. I believe that basketball should be fun but not funny. I don't want players doing things in practice that I don't allow in a game. When Lewis Alcindor triggered the "no-dunk" rule, I did not permit it in practice.

Erickson had great peripheral vision, and he liked to horseplay in drills. He liked to see how far or how high he could throw a ball. He'd watch me out of the corner of his eye and when I'd turn away, he'd try it. He was half hoping I'd see him and chide him. And I suspect that at the same time he was hoping I wouldn't see him, but the other players would. This way he could prove to them he wasn't falling totally into line.

Keith was just the kind of boy I looked for. He gave me fits at times, but when the chips were down and it called for the total effort Keith was ready. And he never was afraid of any other player. If I assigned him to a tough man, he played a much better game. If his man wasn't tough, Keith didn't play as well.

I'll always remember his game against Brigham Young in the 1965 NCAA regionals. He went into the game with a badly pulled groin muscle. It was hard for him to run and jumping really hurt. I gave him Kramer; he did a tremendous job on him and scored 28 points. That's the type of a player Keith was. Give him a stern assignment and he would give a super performance.

I seldom punish players at practice or in front of others. Some coaches believe in giving laps or sprints for errors. I don't think that works. I'm not sure how the body chemistry functions precisely, but I doubt that it responds properly to punishment of that type.

In every facet of basketball, we work on pressure. The opponent provides that during a game. I try to provide it in practice with drills that create game conditions.

I think I thrive on pressure. It has never gotten to me either as a player or a coach. When a player constantly works under pressure, he will respond automatically to it. For this reason I am confident that what the team does on the weekend in a game relates 100 percent to what it does during the week.

Essentially, I'm more of a practice coach than a game coach. This is because of my conviction that a player who practices well, plays well.

17

> *Success is never final.*
> *Failure is never fatal.*
> *It's courage that counts.**

AFTER A FEW years at UCLA, I began to wonder about many facets of my basketball philosophy. We did very well, but except for an "if" or an "and" here and there we might have enjoyed even greater success. I have long contended that there were many earlier years when UCLA might have won an NCAA title if everything had fallen in place like it has in the years since 1964.

At least six or seven times between 1948 and our first title in 1964 we had the talent that could have won the NCAA—not should have, but could have. I've spent hours trying to evaluate where I fell short because the ultimate failure to win must rest with the coach who creates the program and directs the game plan. A lot of things could have fallen into place during those years, but they didn't. Some we had no control over. I had no control over Bill Russell being at the University of San Francisco in 1956 when we had a great club led by Willie Naulls. Russell was the first master of the defensive aspect of college basketball, and when we couldn't match his quickness, height, and desire, we couldn't match USF in points.

Russell later became the most dominant force in pro basketball and was the first of the great intimidators.

---
* Winston Churchill.

I'll never forget one occasion when Willie Naulls, who later played with Bill on the Boston Celtics, going up for a shot, had faked one way and Bill had gone for the fake. Willie went by him, driving for the basket, obviously bent on dunking the ball with both hands.

Just as Willie began to drive the ball down for the dunk, Russell's hand went over the basket. Willie nearly dunked the ball, but Russell blocked the shot. I contended that this was goal tending, but the official insisted the ball never left Naulls' hands.

The move was incredible and surprised everyone so much that no one knew what to call. I think it really shook up our team and probably was the turning point of the game.

Four years earlier, in 1952, I believe we had the talent capable of winning, but we didn't. That was during the Korean War, and freshmen were eligible to play. Two of them, outstanding young players, made the starting five, Don Bragg and Johnny Moore. Bragg was from San Francisco and Moore came from Indiana. Bragg teamed with Jerry Norman at forward while Moore alternated with Mike Hibler at center. We had what I considered an ideal guard combination—the big one in Don Johnson and the little, quick man in Ron Livingston. Both could direct the attack well and understood my game philosophy.

We beat Washington that year for the Pacific Coast Conference title. When we reached the NCAA regionals in Corvallis, Oregon, we ran into a tough Santa Clara team in the first round and were eliminated by a score of 68–59. In the NCAA, every game is a finality. There is no second chance, no double elimination to come back up on the loser's bracket such as there is in the NCAA baseball championship. The fact that Don Bragg, one of our irreplaceables, had broken his big toe when he stumbled coming out of the shower the day before the tournament was small consolation.

You get one shot—and you sink or swim with it. I believe that's the proper system, but it also puts everything in one basket.

Don Johnson and Jerry Norman were co-captains of that 1952 team. Perhaps Norman, more than any other young man, typifies the challenge strong-willed players present to me. Jerry gave me fits. I don't believe I ever had a boy more strong-willed, more sure of himself, and more outspoken.

Jerry was at UCLA when I arrived for the 1948-49 season. Even though he did not play that year, he showed his strong will and temperament in practice. Then, the next year, even though he had been warned to reform, it was necessary for me to dismiss him for insubordination. Jerry was a rebel—very headstrong, set in his ways, and profane. I dismissed him more for profanity than anything else. That I will not tolerate even today. Sure, boys are going to slip during practice and say something. I understand that. But if it continues, I ask them to leave the floor for the day.

Beside profanity, Jerry was obstinate and continued to do things—such as making cross-court passes or using the wrong hand when taking an underbasket shot—that riled me. He was an unselfish player, but I felt that his insubordination undermined the total team effort.

After missing three or four conference games that second year, Jerry came back and apologized to the team and was reinstated. Jerry had a lot of skills potential, and I had convinced myself that one way or the other I was going to get him to come around to my way of doing things. I was sure he was cut out for my style of basketball, and I wasn't going to let him beat me, but, more important, I didn't want him to beat himself. However, it should be mentioned that his close friend Eddie Sheldrake was very instrumental in my giving him another chance.

A strong competitor, full of fire and drive, and with a great innate basketball sense, Jerry ultimately accomplished all the goals I had set for him, and I hope, all of the goals he had set for himself.

By the time Jerry graduated and finished his military obligation, my brother Maurice, the one we called Cat, was principal of West Covina High School in the San Gabriel Valley east of Los Angeles. Cat needed a basketball coach, and upon my recommendation hired Jerry. Later Jerry returned to UCLA as my freshman coach and taught in our Department of Physical Education for the 1957–58 season. And in 1963 he became head varsity assistant.

There were some who wondered about my logic in hiring Jerry, but they didn't know him as I did. He had fine basketball sense and was an excellent recruiter—something I hate doing. And it has always been my contention that anyone who whipped a problem the way Jerry did shows signs of strength. When a person overcomes obstacles, he becomes stronger, and Jerry did that. And he never uses profanity anymore.

I've never wanted a yes man for an assistant. In reality, I guess, I want a rebel—someone who will stand up to me. A man who agrees with you merely inflates your ego and can't be of much help. On the other hand, there must be moderation. I don't want a daily brawl with my assistants. I want to hear their side, their views, their ideas. Some I will adopt, some I will reject, but because of them we will become a better unit.

During my years, I have been fortunate with assistants. Eddie Powell, who came to UCLA with me from South Bend Central and Indiana State, probably knew me better than any of my assistants, and he knew what I wanted done. Bill Putnam, who was Wilbur Johns' aide when I came, stayed on with me until 1963, when he left to go into business. Bill was one of the most loyal, hard-working coaches who ever worked with me. He came to understand me and my ways very well, but his obligations as assistant director of athletics required much of his time.

Doug Sale, who replaced Eddie Powell, would have become outstanding had he stayed with me. He had not played for me and was just learning my ways when he left. There could be no more loyal, determined, nor harder worker than Doug. Denny Crum, who played guard for me in 1958 and 1959 after coming to us from Pierce Junior College, was with me for three years before moving to Louisville as head coach. Like Norman, Crum was a very strong-willed, intense but highly skilled young coach. And Gary Cunningham, who played forward for me, is equally intense. Gary also has a very winning way about him and is destined for an outstanding coaching career. He is an exceptional analyst. Frank Arnold, who joined me after Crum moved to Louisville, is my first non-player assistant since Bill Putnam and Doug Sale.

Every assistant has made a contribution. Some perhaps more than others, but without them the task would be formidable. Several such contributions stand out in my memory, but probably the most famous one came from Norman. That was in the 1967–68 NCAA championships which were played for the first time in the Sports Arena in Los Angeles. We were meeting Houston and Elvin Hayes in the semifinals. This was after we had lost to Houston in the Astrodome, 71–69, in a game in which Lew Alcindor was hardly effective due to an eye injury sustained the week before and in which Elvin Hayes had one of the finest individual performances that I have ever seen.

The Big E, as they called Elvin, believed, if you could accept the press reports, that he could again dominate Alcindor and UCLA. Jerry proposed that we use what is known as a box and one defense. That is a defense tailored to contain one very good player, such as Hayes. I didn't like that because it meant pulling Alcindor out from underneath to one side and would take away from our defensive rebounding. I did not think it wise to take Lewis away from the basket at either end of the court. Furthermore, I was convinced that there was no way that Houston could beat us with Lewis healthy again.

After considerable discussion, we changed the box and one idea to a diamond and one, and we were both pleased. That left Lewis as the point man of the diamond under our defensive basket. I had never used a diamond and one and had used a box and one only on rare occasions. But neither had I worked with a man like Alcindor before, and to repeat, I didn't want to pull him away from either board—ever.

With the diamond and one, Lynn Shackelford became the one. His sole assignment on defense was to shadow Hayes, staying with him even if he went into the stands. Primarily noted for offensive skills, especially that huge rainbow jump shot, Shack did an absolutely amazing job on Hayes, and with support from everyone else, especially Lewis, we literally destroyed a great Houston team, 101–69. I think Shack surprised himself as well as others and followed his assignment to near perfection. Of course, Lewis was always "back there" to help.

Denny Crum helped revise our attack against the zone defense in a way that has proved to be very successful. Many other little things that are difficult to isolate have also been put in thanks to the assistants, especially in the many drills we run every day. Gary Cunningham is a very intelligent contributor and has offered many worthwhile suggestions.

All the assistants over the years have made one important contribution in common. On the bench they are another set of eyes, familiar with what you want to do and able to communicate to the players the little things that may be the difference between victory and defeat. Only one man can make the decisions, but I want all the evidence and information possible before making them. I continually remind myself that I must be open to the various ideas, not bullheaded and stubborn. Each decision must be made through reason, not emotion. Wilfred A. Peterson best illustrates this point in his essay on leadership, "A leader," he said, "is interested in finding the best way—not in having his own way."

In the final years of the 1950s, it was obvious something was not quite right with my basketball philosophy. After we had won 22 and lost 6 in 1956, including the defeat by USF in the Far West Regionals, we went 22 and 4 in 1957, 16 and 10 in 1958, and 16 and 9 in 1959.

Then we started off the '60s by winning 14 and losing 12, the poorest record in my coaching career, except for my first year at Dayton High. A lot of those defeats—Kentucky, Oklahoma State, Purdue, Butler, West Virginia, California—were close, but we were playing basketball, not horseshoes, so close didn't count.

Something was missing. Something was wrong. Something had to be changed, but what? All progress comes through change, and I felt we were not making as much progress as we should. After that 14 and 12 season closed in 1960, I decided to make a total analysis, from recruiting to playing, of everything we did over all the years. Failure is not fatal, but failure to change might be.

18

*A man may make mistakes,
but he isn't a failure
until he starts blaming some
one else.*

TO POINT PRECISELY to any one thing or factor as "the problem" in our not going all the way to an NCAA title is impossible. I can't do it. I don't believe any coach can define to the nth degree why the team succeeded one time and didn't another.

I've always contended that my coaching is done during the week. I don't think basketball is any great strategy game or that it has any master strategists. Admittedly, there is an art to substitution, but there are not too many things that you can change in a game that you haven't prepared for during the week.

Three things are vital to success in basketball—condition, fundamentals, and working together as a team. I said that when I played, I said that when I first started coaching, I said that last year, and I will keep on saying it next year, the year after, and for the rest of my life.

As I tried to put my finger on that one elusive factor that had stood in our way, I went back over every statistical record I had. Only one thing seemed to stand out. Perhaps I worked the players too hard early, and by season's end—or tournament time—they were too worn out to survive the rigors of that level of competition. A related factor seemed equally important. Players on the so-called starting five seemed to practice more together, and when necessity—and injury, foul trouble or fatigue—required a sixth, seventh, or eighth man to go into the game, the new group didn't meld as well together as a team.

Throughout the years, I had always been aware that I should work those top substitutes in with the starting group, but you get so wrapped up in practice you don't do it properly. I want them in there automatically during practice so they are as familiar with the unit as the starting five.

When we began practice in the fall for the 1960-61 season, I had prepared a possible method to accomplish that ideal.

I decided to split the squad of fifteen into two units during the approximate one-third of the practice time we devote to five on five. One unit might consist of seven or eight men, depending on the personnel, the other of the remainder. In other words, if this year I feel we have an eight-man unit that appears to be the core to play most of the games, they'll be in that first group and there will be seven in the second. Next year, it might turn around.

As an example, let's suppose we have three guards like we did in 1971 when we had Henry Bibby, Terry Schofield and Kenny Booker. When we are working five on five, the other guard—let's say it is Booker—is over on the side court shooting free throws. When Booker makes ten free throws he automatically comes over and waits for play to break. When it does, he goes in for Bibby, who will make his free throws and then come in for Schofield. This procedure is repeated throughout the practice.

Instead of going through the motions of making free throws, with this system the players are going to concentrate all the more. The quicker they *make* ten, the quicker they'll get back into the five-on-five action which is our type of scrimmage and which they all enjoy.

Both units and all three positions—guards, forwards, and centers—go through the same procedure. This means that not just the starting five but all of the top seven or eight become very familiar with each other. It also cuts down on the game type contact which the players are under every day. Hopefully, this will stretch their endurance down to those rigorous days of NCAA title play when they will need more energy, drive, and desire.

Since my objective is to keep the rotation going one man at a time, I change the number of free throws the players are required to make. Maybe the guards will make ten, the forwards twelve, the centers seven. That way we won't have two, or even three men, coming in at the same time.

Not only are the players thus more familiar with one another and with working together as a team, but they are more content. This is true not only with the first unit but the second as well. You don't find the thirteenth, fourteenth and fifteenth men being more or less off to themselves and isolated. I believe that this definitely helps them maintain their mental and emotional stability.

Was this rather minute change the reason for our string of successes beginning in 1964? I don't know. It is the only change I have made. We have been in ten out of the last eleven NCAA finals, missing only in 1966. I know I have had teams in other years that have played better basketball, and maybe we've had better material. But I believe material is relative and I believe other teams have had better material, too.

Maybe it just took me a long time to mature as a coach. I don't know.

There is no doubt that a winning tradition gives players more confidence in what the coach is trying to do. They can look back and realize it was right in 1964 and 1965 and might be right now. A fine heritage can enter into the subconscious and enable players to perform to their maximum.

Contrary to what George Allen says, I don't believe they are capable of playing 110 percent or even 100 percent. But they can play closer to 100 percent if they can maintain composure, self-control and endurance. Too much contact work—five on five—seems to take away the competitive edge. By reducing that contact with the rotation of the sixth, seventh and eighth men in those five-on-five sessions, the players won't tire as much in a game late in the season when condition is so vital to the group that sees most of the action.

Selecting those two groups is as difficult as selecting the five that will start the first game. Every man believes he is capable of being in that first unit. If he didn't have that kind of self-confidence, I wouldn't want him on the squad.

That line between first and second unit players is fine indeed. I probably exercise more patience and take more care making those selections than in any other facet of our preparation. Though some of my players may firmly believe I know from day one who will be where, they could not be farther from the truth.

The importance of that so-called sixth man cannot be overestimated. You must have a man who can come off the bench when things are going wrong to get you untracked with a quick basket or two, a sparkling steal that will get your running game going, or so much spirit that it infects the others on the floor. Probably the sixth men best known to the world are some of the pros. Red Auerbach's Boston Celtics may have had two of the greatest in Frank Ramsey and John Havlicek. The latter has also turned out to be a great starter, something you usually don't find in a true sixth man. For years, I have selected a man I believed would be a good sixth man, and in fact, have even recruited sixth men, usually someone who has caught my eye for possessing just the right dynamic qualities.

The kind of man I'm talking about is almost always a highly emotional individual who gets instant adrenalin flowing as soon as you call his name. Kenny Washington, who as a freshman didn't show much promise of making the varsity, is probably the most striking example you could point to from any of the UCLA championship teams. Though he never looked good when he started Kenny was tremendous as a sixth man. Phlegmatic in appearance to the spectators, Kenny seemed to just shuffle onto the floor, but when that ball popped into play, Kenny was off. I can't tell you how many times he came in to hit quick baskets, steal a ball or force an errant pass that resulted in a turnover.

Kenny earned quite a reputation as the sixth man at UCLA, especially when we won in 1964 and 1965, when he came off the bench to ignite us against Duke and Michigan, but he was just as capable in 1966 when we didn't make the NCAA.

Another great one was Fred Crabtree, who played for UCLA in 1956–57. Although Fred gave up basketball after his sophomore season and transferred to Cal at Berkeley, he was one of our most valuable players. He came to us with fine credentials, living up to them in fine style that one year, with 163 points in 25 games for a 6.5 average. Statistics, however, never reflect the true value of a sixth man. Fred was one of the best I ever had.

19

It is what you learn after you know it all that counts.

It seemed to take almost two years for things to jell with our new practice regime. I know we were better because of it in 1960–61, when we were 18 and 8 but only second in the Pacific Eight Conference. The next year, 1961–62, I feel the change really began to pay off. We won the conference with a 10 and 2 record, beat Utah State 73–62 in the first round of the NCAA Far West Regions and Oregon State 88–69 for the right to go to the final round of four in Louisville.

We lost to Cincinnati in the semifinals 72–70, but we just as easily could have won. I have never been more proud of a winning team than I was of this team, even in losing. As is often the case, they were equal in every way to the Cincinnati team that won. The line between champion and challenger is fine.

Many of our teams over the years have been good enough to win, but didn't. Just as with this one things didn't fall in place. That's why I feel so fortunate for the record we have compiled in NCAA play during the last decade.

There is no doubt that the talent was present in 1961–62. We had three seniors—Gary Cunningham and Pete Blackman at forwards and Johnny Green at guard—plus two fine sophomores, Fred Slaughter at center and Walt Hazzard at guard. Though our season got off to a slow start these fine young men meshed together as the season progressed and came within an eyelash of being our first champions. After letting Cincinnati build up an early lead, our team made a courageous comeback to tie the score at the half. The second half was close all the way with Thacker of Cincinnati hitting from outside in the final second to win it. Ironically, it was his only basket of the game.

The talent was present. Maybe the coaching still lacked something. Who knows? I don't. I know that fine group of boys played their hearts out all season long. And they had fun, too, but within my bounds. They were all definite, different personalities who respected one another, jelled together as the season rolled on, and became a strong, strong team.

I've always liked fierce competitors who play with the desire and determination necessary to enhance some natural ability. One of that type whose play I have always admired, even when I might be yelling to the officals about it, was Ken Stanley of USC. Similar in some respects to Curtis Rowe, one of my championship players of whom I am very fond, Ken was not spectacular—just a strong, consistent, all-around fine player and tough competitor.

Rugged, tough, hard-nosed competitors like Stanley, Bill McClintock of California, and Ckervinko of Arizona State have always appealed to me. They were living proof that players can be aggressive without being dirty. And you could always guarantee they would play the same, steady, almost flawless game against UCLA. Dick Banton, Jack Hirsch, and John Green should be singled out along with Curtis Rowe and some others as UCLA players of that breed. They seldom got the credit they truly deserved.

I had seen positive signs in 1961–62 that the change in the practice regime was showing. When replacements came in they showed their familiarity with the others. We had greater unity, greater rapport between players and consequently a better team. Now to fit in with Slaughter and Hazzard, who were the only starters back in 1962–63, came two jaycee transfers, Keith

Erickson and Jack Hirsch. They were to play dominant roles the next two seasons for UCLA along with two fine guards, Freddie Goss and Gail Goodrich.

In a matter of days, I realized that those five plus Jim Milhorn, Kim Stewart, and Dave Waxman appeared to have the skills, speed, and desire to use a zone press as the basic defense. I had always had in the back of my head that with the right personnel it could be devastating at our level as it had been for me at Indiana State and in high school. As a matter of fact I had started out to use it several times and then decided not to. Early the year before, it hadn't worked too well, so I junked it; in restrospect, I think far too soon. Now, I told myself, I've got a young team that appears to have the qualities necessary to make it work, and I'm staying with it. I did not announce my intention to the squad, however.

Previously, I had used the zone press at UCLA only in certain situations—never as the primary defensive weapon. Not having really worked with the idea of using it full time since I left Indiana State, I decided this year it was basic. I was determined we would sink or swim with the press, rather than having to look back with regret for abandoning it. This time we would give it a fair test.

By the middle of the season, there was no question in my mind these boys could make it go. They began to destroy people with scoring blitzes that literally ended the games. Sooner or later it got to every opponent. The 2-2-1 basic zone press certainly built confidence in our overall game.

Once again we won the conference but got beat in the NCAA tournament by an amazingly red-hot Arizona State team at Provo 93-79. The fact that we lost the consolation to USF, 76-75, doesn't matter. Because I do not like consolation games, I play everyone, especially seniors and those who haven't played too much before. In my opinion the only time when a consolation game has any merit is in a preseason or holiday tournament when you can work on things that need it. I firmly believe you should never end the season with a consolation game.

As we flew home from Provo, dejected to a certain extent, I also had a great amount of confidence for the year to come. Everyone would be back, everyone who had made the press go and our fast-break offense work so well in going 20 and 9. We would be a year older, a year more mature, and I believed then that the 1963-64 season could be the ultimate success that I had predicted in my verse to Pete Blackman.

That first championship is always something special. This one pleased me greatly for two other reasons. Not only was it the first, but it truly established the zone press defense as an offensive weapon. And it was won by the smallest team, comparatively speaking, ever to attain that goal. Those boys, anchored by Keith Erickson in the number five spot, made it a slashing, dangerous, destructive force that probably earned more time and space in the sports news for UCLA basketball than anything before.

Though I have often been asked to name an all-time team of players I've coached, I never have and never will. It is less difficult, however, to answer a similar question about such a dominant force in our success as the 2-2-1 zone press defense. Many people have asked me who I think would make the best composite of my players for this sole assignment.

Two can be selected rather quickly. Erickson would be number five man. This takes a special type of player. He must be quick, alert, courageous, and unselfish; able to read the man with the ball and very good at handling defense when outnumbered. But, most important, he must be able to make that instant decision to fly forward from his safety spot and attempt the steal of the long pass without fear of failure. Keith possessed every one of those attributes, mainly because he loved a challenge.

The number five man is the last man. Some call him the safety man, the safety valve, or the anchor man. He is the deepest man towards our basket and the last defender if our opponents break the press. I call him *the director*. Every man on the team must listen to him.

The number one man plays to the left of the basket the opponent is defending and harasses the inbound pass. One of the masters at this task was Gail Goodrich. Because of his boyish looks and because of his size (at 6' 1" he was the shortest and smallest of the starters on the 1964 and 1965 champions), he fooled many. But Gail played a lot bigger than his size and, like Erickson, was an intense competitor. He had exceedingly long arms, a factor that made him an ideal number one man because so many players trying to inbound the ball didn't realize how wide those arms could spread. Gail turned many a pass into a steal and, often, into an unassisted basket.

For the number two spot playing alongside Gail and to the right of the basket our opponent defends would be Keith Wilkes. A highly intelligent player with a fine grasp of the game, he has extremely quick hands, instant reflexes, and stands tall at 6' 6". So fluid was he in his movements that he too caught a lot of people by surprise. Many loose balls were tipped off his hands and captured by the mid-court pair.

The number three man—and I want to emphasize that these selections are solely for the 2-2-1 press and nothing else—would be the late Walt Torrence. The three spot is behind Goodrich and a bit inside his right foot. Torrence, who played for UCLA in 1957-58-59 as a guard, stood 6' 3" and was as quick as any man I have coached. He had great anticipation and was especially adept at coming forward to tip a ball away on an inbound pass while still playing tight on any man working his assigned zone. Walt was killed a few years back in an auto accident up in the San Joaquin Valley.

Number four has to be Sidney Wicks. Here is a man who measures 6' 8" plus, with the agility, quickness and speed of a 6 footer. The number four spot is located to the right of the number three man as you face the end line and just inside and back of the number two man. Wicks played the number five spot in his brilliant years, but he is an ideal number four because of his range, quickness, and ability to handle both the quicker, smaller man who will be back trying to help the inbound man get the ball in play and the big men coming back to help out. Few big men are as quick as Wicks. Jack Hirsch at 6′ 3″ also played this spot exceptionally well.

That's almost an ideal 2–2–1 press unit. It's not my all-star team. It's not the best team offensively nor the best in total defense, but I believe it could more than hold its own with anyone playing the 2–2–1 press.

All of the team have been well known to college basketball since we began our string of championships in 1964 except perhaps Torrence. I think it is obvious that Walt must have been a very talented young man to rate my choice for the number three spot.

It is a formidable unit, one I would like to be able to put on the floor in any game, in any year, just to play the press. Each man could have been a master of his assigned duties. Each was well suited to meld in with the others, and Erickson was a master director. As the only man with a full view of the floor and what is taking place, the number five man is indispensable. Keith, who possessed that innate sense of when to charge and when to fall back on a long down-court pass, commanded the press with great effectiveness.

I always caution my safety man never to go for the interception unless he can get it. But though he must never guess, he can't just sit back and wait. He must have the courage to fly forward. He can't hesitate. If he does, it's too late. Erickson never lacked for courage and he seldom made an error in judgment.

It is quite possible that Bill Walton ultimately may challenge Erickson for that all-important "directorship of the press," or number five spot. He was so tremendous as a sophomore.

20

*Enjoy the present hour,
be mindful of the past;
And neither fear nor wish
the approaches of the last.*

AFTER WE HUNG that first NCAA championship banner in 1964, there was considerable speculation whether we could join Oklahoma State, Kentucky, USF and Cincinnati to win back-to-back NCAA titles. We had the number five and number one men back in Erickson and Goodrich, plus Freddie Goss, Doug McIntosh, and Kenny Washington as well as two fine young sophomores in Edgar Lacey and Mike Lynn.

I believed we could. My prime concern was complacency. Many fine clubs had tried to win back-to-back titles but only four had succeeded since the NCAA began in 1939. I was convinced we had found the makings of a formula of success. The constant rotation of players into the floor unit in practice plus the arrival of the zone press seemed to be the answer, but one successful season doesn't make a career.

No one is more aware than the coach that every year marks a change in circumstances. With the graduation of young men who have established you as something of a success or a failure, depending on the season, new problems or opportunities present themselves in the form of new personnel and manpower grouping. My basic concepts, nevertheless, have remained the same.

One of them, having to do with time-outs, is almost a fetish with me. I value time-outs like gold, and I guard them with the same zeal Uncle Sam does Ft. Knox. I try to use them with great care and conserve them to the final minutes.

Never do I want to call the first time-out in a game. Once the game tempo has been established, or if we are making a big run at an opponent, or even if we are behind, I prefer not to be the first to interrupt the game, under almost any circumstance. But I have.

Why not call the first time-out? First among several factors is condition. I have always told my teams that we are going to be in better condition than the other team and we want our opponents to need time-outs for a rest. I don't say I think we are going to be in better condition or we are going to try to be. I say we are going to be in better condition, a positive statement.

Being in better condition pays dividends if you can put the pressure on an opponent and keep it on, both offensively and defensively. This does not necessarily have to be done with a pressing defense. A tight pressure defense may serve the same purpose, providing, of course, that we are constantly and continuously applying offensive pressure also. I constantly repeat the admonition I learned from Piggie Lambert at Purdue: "The team that makes the most mistakes will probably win." There is much truth in that statement if you analyze it properly. The doer makes mistakes, and I want doers on my team—players who make things happen.

Ninety percent of the time the game is going to be decided in the final five minutes. When two teams are evenly matched, the better conditioned team will usually execute better when fatigue sets in, and will probably win. And if you have all your time-outs remaining, you can use them strategically to your advantage in the game situation.

Occasions when I have called the first time-out are few indeed, averaging no more than once a season. But I have done so in some pretty crucial games and at critical points where I felt a time-out was mandatory.

One of the most important came in the 1964 NCAA finals against Duke University in Kansas City. They had us down and were killing our press by getting through it to hit the jump shot. I was afraid our players might lose confidence, even though they hadn't all year long. Not wanting that to happen, I called time, reiterating that I wanted them to stay with the pressing defense; that Duke, although shooting exceedingly well, would ultimately start missing, and the press would turn the game around.

In the next four minutes or so we established our tempo and caught them at 27 all. Then *they* called time. After they got three points on three consecutive free throws we broke the game apart and ran the score out to 41–30, when they called time again.

It was our pressure defense that broke Duke's stability. First taking its toll mentally, it had finally done so physically as well. And that is what we seek to do—keep the pressure on, never letting up and always staying aware that pressure comes not only from the zone press defense but from every other thing we do. That's why I am so reluctant to call that initial time-out, or, for that matter, almost any time-out.

The next time I called time-out first was a full year later, in the 1965 NCAA championship against Michigan at the Portland Coliseum. It wasn't as critical this time, but our play was a little too loose and sloppy. After about five minutes Michigan was ahead by three points, and I wanted to tighten things up. My instructions: get a little more discipline, give Keith Erickson a little more help on Cazzie Russell, hit Edgar Lacey from the high post, set the double for Goodrich, tighten our press, and things would be all right. In a few minutes we turned things around, and captured the lead 26–24. Michigan called time with 8:56 to play. In the minutes remaining we outscored them 21 to 10 and left the floor ahead 47–34 at the half with the game in command.

There are many who disagree with me about my fetish of not taking the first time-out, but I consider my logic to be sound. Almost every time that I have felt it was an absolute necessity to call that first time-out it has been beneficial. I can't say every time because I can't recall every one, but it helped us win in 1964 and 1965 in the NCAA finals, and it worked in 1970 against Jacksonville. It is true, however, that there may have been times when I should have called one and didn't. Perhaps I could have broken the tempo at Arizona State in the NCAA regionals in 1963 and prevented our defeat.

Against Jacksonville at Cole Fieldhouse on the University of Maryland campus, we had played 6 minutes 52 seconds when I signaled for a time-out. Behind 14–6, we had hit only two for seven from the field while Jacksonville was seven for twelve, but I was concerned more with the defense than with Jacksonville's fantastic shooting percentage, a result of our giving up easy shots. I did not feel our players were giving them proper respect.

We had started with a defense I was convinced should work against Jacksonville, with Sidney Wicks against Artis Gilmore. I didn't care that Gilmore was over 7 feet and Wicks only 6' 8". There should be no way in which Jacksonville could lob the ball over Sidney. If Sidney could stand behind a 7 footer and get the ball or go up and block a shot on the turn, Sidney should be able to keep Gilmore from getting the ball if he is alert and playing in front. Of course, we needed help from the weak side, but Curtis Rowe was very good at that.

But it was obvious from the bench that Sidney was concerned about the defense after Gilmore got one on him. I didn't want Sidney being concerned about anything but being Sidney and playing like only Sidney could play, so I called a time-out and changed things a bit. Little by little we whittled away at their lead, getting it down to 36–32 with 3.03 to play in the half. Once again condition told when we ran away from them with nine straight points to end the half 41–36.

Going back to back in 1964 and 1965—after losing three starters the second year—was a tribute to the players. Even so, we went into the 1964–65 season with what I thought might be nearly as good a team. Because we had two highly stable, highly talented starters back—Goodrich, the number one man in the zone press, and Erickson, the safety man at number five—we decided to alter our zone press from the 2–2–1 that had carried us to that perfect year. Instead we went with a 1–2–1–1 almost all year long. We didn't have the really big man such as Oklahoma State had with Bob Kurland in 1945 and 1946 or USF had with Bill Russell in 1955 and 1956 to help us repeat. But we had fine range coupled with speed and quickness and I believed we had an excellent chance. Furthermore, I felt that the change to the 1–2–1–1 might cause confusion to our opponents who were expecting the 2–2–1.

That chance was almost obliterated in our first game. We went into Champaign-Urbana to meet Illinois in its new 17,000-seat Assembly Hall. We ran into a bunch of real sharpshooters. They had a tremendous game. Their fine ball handling, quick moves, and excellent outside jump shooting enabled them to work with great success against our press. They had a tremendous shooting percentage the first half. I know I didn't call the first time-out even though Illinois couldn't miss. From the bench I kept assuring the boys to play their game, Illinois had to cool off.

Only they didn't. They shot nearly 70 percent for the game. We were never close. And there wasn't much we could do about it. It was probably the worst lacing of my coaching career, a 27-point difference. We scored 83 points—which will win most ball games—but Illinois scored 110. It was no fluke. We just got slashed to bits. I told the team the next morning not to worry about it. It was true we could no longer match the undefeated performance of the year before but we were a very good ball club, and could settle down to do very well. With the pressure of a long winning streak gone, we could play our game.

The boys seemed to understand because the

next night at Indiana State we scored a runaway win, 112–76. We rolled right along until the holiday when we went into Chicago Stadium to meet Iowa and Loyola of Chicago on consecutive nights. Then the Hawkeyes got to us, 87–82.

The raking by Illinois and the loss to Iowa were the only ones that year. Every player we had made a unique contribution to our second winning season. Seniors Erickson and Goodrich were superplayers, and sophomores Lacey and Lynn fit in very well with such veterans as center Doug McIntosh, guard Freddie Goss, and sixth man Ken Washington. Lacey, a very intent, sometimes moody young man, was highly skilled on the backboards despite his lack of weight. Lynn, on the other hand, was a rugged, boyish appearing youngster who had a deceptively quick pair of hands. Freddie Goss gave us fine outside shooting and endless hustle, McIntosh gave us good solid play at center, and Kenny Washington again was a tremendous sixth man. Quite naturally, however, it was Erickson and Goodrich who were constant sparks. What a pair they were!

Kenny Washington, who has to rank with the great sixth men in college basketball, seemed to thrive on supertough competition. The two greatest games of his career came in the NCAA championships in 1964 and 1965. A man truly shows his mettle in games like those. To go in under that kind of pressure and deliver, as Kenny did both years—that's a great sixth man.

Against Duke in the 1964 finals, Kenny went in early in the first half at forward and remained to score 26 points—his all-time high at UCLA—and get 12 rebounds. We were ahead 17–15, but fighting to stay even, when he made his first free throw, ending up with 9 points in the first half. But what he did to Duke in that second half was something else. When he wasn't hitting his jump shot, he was driving by his man for a lay-in or charging the boards for a tip-in, or making a mid-court steal to set up the fast break.

The next year against Michigan, Kenny was superb

again. We were behind, 20–13, when in seconds he hit two jumpers to close the gap and then tied the game at 24 all with another one from the top of the key. Once again, cast as that vital sixth man, Washington was everywhere, blending in his fine shooting touch with his speed and skill. Working in harmony with his teammates, he sparked us to really destroy a great Michigan team led by Cazzie Russell. Washington scored 17 points in relief of the injured Erickson but the life he gave us was as instrumental in our victory as his points.

Although it was truly a team victory, the brilliant play of Gail Goodrich in that 1965 championship will never be forgotten either. Few players will ever play as well under such championship pressure. He and Keith Erickson, the only two returning starters from the 1964 champions, were both inspirational floor leaders. Gail responded to the added burden placed on him by Erickson's injury with a performance that easily made him the most valuable player of the tournament in my eyes. The record books show that his 42 points were his all-time high—this in his last collegiate game and for the national championship against a powerful team. What can never be measured statistically—his take-charge confidence and spirited floor leadership—was equally important.

We might not have had our NCAA string broken in 1966, when we failed to win the conference, if we hadn't lost Lacey and Goss for the season. We looked like a very solid club going in with Lacey and Lynn at forwards; McIntosh, now a senior, at center; and Goss teaming with Mike Warren, a brilliant young sophomore from my old high school, South Bend Central, at guard; plus that number six man—Washington. Edgar sustained a knee injury, we never knew how, but he was never again the Edgar Lacey that we had known. Eventually he had to have surgery, was forced to lay off a year, and never came back to the brilliance we all expected of him. Goss was ill off and on all year, and though Warren was an excellent young sophomore, he needed the stabilizing influence of Goss. We ended up second in the conference (10 and 4), 18 and 8 overall for the year, and as spectators for the NCAA.

21

Dare to be a Daniel!
Dare to stand alone!
Dare to have a purpose firm!
*Dare to make it known.**

ON TUESDAY, May 4, 1965, at Power Memorial High School in New York City, Lewis Alcindor announced that he would attend UCLA. With that announcement, the basketball world automatically declared that UCLA would be the first in history to win three NCAA titles in a row.

Up to that point in time, I had never seen Lewis play. He had visited UCLA the first week in April. As he returned to International Airport he indicated that he would enroll in the fall. About a week later he asked if I would come to New York to meet his parents. Jerry Norman, then my assistant, and I flew East where we met with Lewis and his parents for about an hour—at one o'clock in the morning because Lewis's father worked the four to midnight shift.

They, like Lewis, wanted their son to go to a university with high academic standing as well as a good basketball program. We felt UCLA met those requirements and we certainly wanted a young man of such talent and of such high intelligence. We were also realists. We knew that every university in America was after him. He had scholarship offers from every major college, and we felt the great distance to Los Angeles would pretty well rule out his coming to us.

---

*P. P. Bliss, "Dare to Be a Daniel!"

After he announced his choice of UCLA, we began to hear all kinds of stories about how we had used the late Jackie Robinson, one of UCLA's greatest athletes ever; the late Dr. Ralph Bunche, a former Bruin basketball player, who was with the United Nations in New York; and Willie Naulls of the New York Knickerbockers, an All-American for us in 1956, to recruit Lewis.

If Jackie Robinson ever talked to Lewis about UCLA, he did it on his own. Jackie never talked to me about it. Dr. Bunche did contact Lewis. He wrote Lewis a letter, with a copy to me, about Lewis's coming to UCLA, in which he said that at UCLA Lewis would have an equal opportunity, the basketball would be good, and the academics good. I would never presume to have a man of Dr. Bunche's stature call on a basketball prospect. That he did so on his own is something for which I have been forever grateful.

Willie Naulls was definitely working to get Lewis to UCLA. The Knicks, in those days, practiced in the Power Memorial Gym once in a while. But I never really believed we had much of a chance at getting this great young man who ranked, as a prospect, with the likes of Wilt Chamberlain, Jerry Lucas, and Oscar Robertson.

Today Lewis Alcindor is Kareem Abdul-Jabbar. The Chamberlains, Lucases, and Robertsons—all of basketball recognize him by the name he has legally taken. While I accept this change in keeping with his faith and try to honor his request that I call him Kareem, I continually find myself using the name by which I knew him so well. And I am sure that his parents have the same problem, perhaps to an even greater degree. Try as I may, this fine young man will always be Lewis Alcindor to me. I hope he will understand my using the name by which we all knew him at that time in describing the years he spent with us.

Lewis was one of a kind. I hadn't really expected to get him, and, even after he made the announcement, I wondered if he would really show up in September for classes.

Actually, Lewis was no stranger to UCLA as a player or a person. When Lewis was a junior in high school, I spoke at the Valley Forge Basketball Clinic in Philadelphia. His coach, Jack Donohue, wrote that he was going to attend the clinic and would like to talk to me some time during it about "his big fellow." We did talk. I did express a great interest and I did tell him that if it were at all possible, UCLA would like to be the last school Lewis would visit during his senior year. I believe that is how it ultimately worked out.

After Lewis's sophomore season in high school, Edgar Lacey, who had been such a great player for Jefferson High in Los Angeles, was picked on the *Parade* magazine prep All-American, as was Lewis. Edgar and Lewis met for the first time when the team appeared on the Ed Sullivan show in New York. That summer, Edgar went to the Catskill Mountains in New York to work and play summer basketball, and so did Lewis.

There was no doubt in my mind of Lewis's potential. If there was doubt of any kind, it was in my ability to live up to the forecasts that were immediately made: three straight NCAAs, no defeats—things like that. I didn't know exactly how I could use a big man to the best advantage. I had never had the chance to experiment. All I had were ideas, but with no valid way to determine whether they were sound or not. All the concepts that I believed would work when you had a big man needed one in order for me to find out.

What Lewis could do and how he could dominate a game was instantly obvious at his first practice as a freshman. And after the first game, there was no doubt that my theories would work with the big man, especially such a fantastic big man.

As his first varsity season approached, UCLA was hit with two major losses in experienced personnel. Edgar Lacey, with whom Lewis roomed when he first came to UCLA, never got over his knee injury of the year before. When finally surgery was necessary, Edgar was lost for the year. And Mike Lynn, who had teamed with Edgar so well at forward or center, was lost through disciplinary action of the university.

We went into the season with four starting sophomores and one junior. Probably as young a team as any major college had ever put on the floor was burdened with living up to the press's forecast that they would be the national champions. Lewis, of course, was the center. Lynn Shackelford, a 6' 5" sophomore from Burbank, was one forward, and Kenny Heitz, a 6' 3" product of Righetti High in Santa Maria who was recruited as a guard or possibly a sixth man, was at the other wing.

Our only varsity experience rested with Mike Warren, a small but gifted player from South Bend Central. He was as smart and valuable a guard as I had ever had. Mike was a junior. Going with him was Lucius Allen, a 6'2" All-State guard from Wyandotte High in Kansas City, Kansas. Allen had almost the same kind of potential at guard as did Alcindor at center.

Still, there was concern and skepticism in my mind whether what I wanted to do with these youngsters was right, whether it would take full advantage of Lewis's potential greatness.

In this, my first chance to build around an outstanding big man, I scrapped my whole offense and went to a totally different one than I had ever used. A complete low post offense placed the center deep, near the basket and well inside the free throw line. I had used a double post, a double low post, a double high post in a limited way, but never a single low post. To take full advantage of his height, I wanted Lewis Alcindor no farther from the offensive basket than he could reach. I almost wanted him to be able to stick his arm out and dunk the ball—no more than eight feet away.

I had spent literally hundreds of hours from the time Lewis entered UCLA as a freshman and the beginning of his sophomore year in 1967 talking to coaches whom I respected about the low post offense, diagramming plays and analyzing the consequences and trying to determine just how this seven foot plus youngster would fit in with the others.

The fit was instantly obvious. We opened the season against USC with an easy win and then decisively defeated a strong Duke team on consecutive nights, 88-54 and 107-87.

Immediately, the press again predicted the perfect season, the NCAA title, everything. Sometimes I wondered if they even expected our opposition to score a basket. It was well recognized that Shackelford's forte was shooting. He was not an outstanding all-around basketball player, but as a pure shooter he was something else, especially from the corner. If his defensive man floated in on Lewis, it meant that Shack would get not only more shots but more of them open shots. On the other hand, if the defense came out on Shackelford, then Lewis would have more freedom underneath.

Kenny Heitz, our other forward, was a quick, driving player with good speed. The fact that he had to wear glasses on the floor did not keep him from being tough on defense and an adequate shooter. Neither forward was a superstar, but they were solid, dependable youngsters who played it my way. When you coupled them with the super super in Alcindor and one of the greatest guard combines—Warren and Allen—that I have ever coached, it was a formidable squad.

There was little question after that first weekend against archrival USC that we were going to be some kind of an offensive force. There was still a large question about our defense. Once again I was confronted with the same question: how do you play it with that big man with such fine reactions, great anticipation, and great desire?

I had long had a cardinal defensive rule that a forward should never give up the baseline at the end of the court and allow a man to slip through the back door to the basket. Where always before we had tried to drive people away from the basket, away from the baseline, now it was a different story. We wanted them to drive on Lewis. We wanted our forwards to freelance more on defense, gamble more, take more chances. With Lewis underneath, we could do it with a certain degree of safety.

I also decided after a game or two that we would not be the greatest fast-break team I had ever had, nor would we use the zone press as much. It was obvious we were not going to be as adept at that as I thought, although Lewis had great speed and was a lot quicker and niftier than many believed. But we were so strong with both our set offense and set defense that I decided not to make the press a basis of our defense and to fast-break only when Lewis could outlet the ball for a definite and obvious advantage.

It was a great year. We won the Pac Eight. We won the NCAA, beating Dayton in Louisville, 79–64. But the most impressive thing was that we were undefeated in thirty games with four sophomores and an average team age of 19.1 years—the youngest ever to win the NCAA and the youngest ever to go undefeated.

The season was not without problems, nonetheless. Lewis Alcindor was always being challenged, and not only on the court by our opponents. His mere presence created problems among society in general and even among his teammates, for neither of which could Lewis be held responsible. Some of our players objected to the tremendous amount of space he received in newspapers and magazines and on radio and television. I recognized this and tried to avoid it as much as possible. Mostly, however, I tried to get the point across that Lewis's mere presence at UCLA was going to get all of our players far more publicity than they could possibly get otherwise. It made good sense for them not to be envious and jealous of the attention being paid to Lewis, especially since he was personally unselfish and deserving of all credit he would receive.

All our boys were fine players who worked exceptionally well together and made an ideal team. At the same time, it was obvious that Kenny Heitz at 6′ 3″ wouldn't be starting at forward on such a strong team unless there were an Alcindor in there. Shackelford was not a driver so he needed an Alcindor to open up his jump shot from the corner. Their abilities, fortunately, fit in well with what we had. Warren and Allen, by contrast, were an exceptional pair of guards who ranked with the Hazzard-Goodrich and Vallely-Bibby pairs. They would fit in with any team, but not our forwards as a pair.

While the problems with the squad were minimal and were more often than not resolved within our team, it was entirely human that there should be difficult moments. A few times they spilled out when some players complained to the press. Once a couple of them charged that I gave Lewis special privileges, which is true, to a degree. They also knew that I never treated them all alike in every respect and never professed that I would. However, they needed to accept my concept of trying to give each individual the treatment that he earned and deserved.

Another gripe was that Lewis got two glasses of orange juice for breakfast and they only got one. True. But they didn't mention that Lewis didn't eat anything else. They said he often got to room alone. True. He often did. But they didn't mention that you couldn't get two king-size beds in a room, and that was when he roomed alone. Once in a while Lewis would have a migraine headache. Having had them myself, I know how they affect your ability to function. I would tell him to go into the training room, take a pillow, turn off the lights and lie down. If he felt like coming back to practice, fine. If he felt he would be better at home, go home. He'd lie down. He'd never leave. Often he'd come back to practice. I would do the same for any other boy with migraines, but some players considered this preferential treatment.

Lewis took the most unfair raps, however, from the public. The signing of autographs was a major problem not only for Lewis but for the team. I remember one time when he must have signed thirty or forty autographs before I came out from the dressing room.

"Lewis," I said, "that's enough. We're keeping the rest of the team waiting." Little kids were running after him trying to get his signature.

One of the adults commented, "Look at that big ———, too good to sign an autograph."

They didn't know he had already signed thirty or forty and that I had told him to board the bus.

On another occasion, when we were walking more or less together, some lady remarked, "Look at that big black freak."

I heard it. I was two or three feet from Lewis and I know he heard it. I tried to explain to him that she didn't mean to be rude, that his size did startle people, and that it had nothing to do with his race.

"Do you think, coach," he asked, "if Mel Counts [a 7' plus center at Oregon State and in the NBA] walked in she would have said 'Look at that big white freak'?"

"No, Lewis, she wouldn't, but that is part of the basic society."

We discussed the incident at length and I could see his point. "I understand your situation, Lewis," I said, "I think."

"Coach," he replied, "I think you would be as understanding as any white man that I have ever known, but there is no way you can really understand. You are white, I am black. You are 5 feet 10 inches tall and I am 7 feet."

That was another of the problems. How tall was Alcindor? I was asked that once a day for four years. I gave everyone the same answer, 7' 1⅝", but no one ever believed me. I don't think they would believe me if they stood beside the yardstick while he was measured.

I can say without equivocation that in the four years Lewis Alcindor played for me at UCLA his mere presence created problems that shouldn't have existed, but the young man himself personified cooperation as exemplified by his greatness on the basketball floor. He was the least demanding of any superstar I have ever known. In fact, he should never have been held responsible for the problems that seemed to surround him. Such tremendous ability often brings out petty jealousy and envy from both teammates and opponents.

22

*A gentleman is one who considers the rights of others before his own feelings,
And the feelings of others before his own rights.*

LEWIS FERDINAND ALCINDOR, JR., was, in my opinion, the finest truly big man ever to play basketball up to his time. He could do anything you asked of him, and do it almost to perfection. His tremendous physical ability, however, could not have been nearly so effective had it not been for his intelligence and exceptional emotional control. Seldom would he strike back in anger despite the fact he took more of a physical beating in his three years of basketball at UCLA than anyone I have ever seen.

The ability to keep his emotions under control was as much responsible for our winning three successive NCAA championships in the so-called Alcindor era as anything else. He had total control of a ten to fifteen foot circle around his position on the floor. He completely intimidated opposing players merely by the threat of moving out to meet them when they were driving toward the basket.

Lewis probably could get higher in the air than any man of his size. I don't think his timing was quite so good as Bill Russell's, but it was excellent nonetheless. It's almost impossible to make an objective comparison of men who played their collegiate ball more than ten years apart.

Russell was the first of the great intimidators at the defensive end of the floor, while Lewis was the first of the great intimidators at both ends. They were completely alike in one most important attribute: everything they did was subordinated to the team.

Russell was tremendous on defense. People have forgotten that at USF he was also excellent on offense and scored more points than they can remember. But there was a wide difference between Russell and Alcindor at the offensive end. Lewis possessed a fine touch and was such a beautiful jumper that he could shoot either straight in or off the glass. His hook was also excellent and, although our style didn't really permit him to use it going to the base line, he became very proficient at using it in deep across the lane. Most people weren't aware of his hook at UCLA, but it was pretty good.

Lewis was really more like Wilt Chamberlain than Russell in all-around ability. He was more maneuverable than Wilt but not nearly so powerful. Had Wilt been surrounded by the playing cast that Russell was with the Boston Celtics, and had he had a Red Auerbach as coach, his team might well have won all those championships. Suffice it to say that Bill, Wilt, and Lewis all belong among the all-time greats.

One of Lewis's impressive statistics is that of the 88 games he played for us, in 87 he shot at least 50 percent from the floor. The only game in which he fell below that was in our loss to Houston at the Astrodome—when he had vertical double vision in the eye that had been scratched at Cal two weeks before. His three-year shooting percentages were 64.9, 61.6 and 63.5

For only the second time in my coaching career, in 1967-68 all five starters were back from the year before. In addition, we had two other outstanding starters from our 1964-65 champions, Edgar Lacey and Mike Lynn, competing for starting positions. Both expected to be starters automatically. There was no way, however, that I would move men back who had started all season the year before for two men who had been forced to sit out the year.

Lacey and Lynn were going to have to work their

way into that first unit. Physically they were good enough, probably better than either Heitz or Shackelford. But Edgar, gifted as he was two years before when he was hurt, was never able to regain his form—physically, mentally, or emotionally. Lynn was capable, but when the two joined as a combine, a harmonious relationship and desirable team play became impossible.

I moved Heitz back to guard, a more normal position for him, and alternated Shackelford, Lynn, and Lacey at forwards for awhile. I was trying to find the strongest line-up, not appease Lynn and Lacey. If I had not had Alcindor both of them would have been in the line-up, but Lewis and Shackelford complemented each other so well that I felt Shack deserved to be there.

The line-up was almost a juggling act for the first thirteen games. Then came the big scene in the Astrodome, with the largest crowd ever to see a college basketball game and an even larger crowd watching on coast-to-coast television. "The Big A," as someone wrote, "versus The Big E." But it really wasn't. Alcindor was just half of himself because of his injured eye. He had been in a dark room and had not practiced in over a week. Lewis at far below par, however, was still a potent psychological force. His mere physical presence forced opponents to alter their game—both offensively and defensively.

It had not been an easy year, as most would have supposed. The internal problems of having too many standouts had confirmed my long-time conviction that if you have more than seven or eight players who could be considered starters you may be breeding discontent. All this in spite of the fact we were going along undefeated, were physically very strong, and had the best bench ever.

But the Astrodome ended our streak of wins and, much to my concern, the playing career at UCLA of Edgar Lacey.

I started Edgar and gave him probably the toughest

assignment possible—playing Elvin Hayes. Going in, I was concerned about Hayes. Maybe there was no way Edgar or anyone else could have contained him. I didn't think anyone could but I wanted Hayes played a certain way and Edgar wasn't doing that. I had asked him to play Hayes high on the side to prevent his receiving the ball. If he reversed for a pass, he would be running into Alcindor, and I did not think he would like that. If Edgar had played Elvin that way and Elvin had scored at will, I would have allowed him to try his way. But Edgar didn't try what I had told him to do, so I pulled him and put in Jim Nielsen, a 6′ 7″ reserve who had size and determination but nowhere near the skills of Edgar.

Early in the second half, I told Jerry Norman to get Edgar ready. "Look at him, coach," said Jerry. I surveyed the bench and saw Edgar at the far end, head down, not watching the game, really hanging, so I didn't put him back in. We lost, 71–69. Afterwards, I was asked by reporters why I had not played Edgar in the second half. "Edgar didn't give me the impression," I told the press, "that he wanted to play. He told me he could not handle Hayes and that was the reason."

That was in the papers, and Edgar was upset. But he had taken it wrong, somehow, because every man who has ever played for me knows that I demand attention to the game from those on the bench. They must be ready when they are called. Edgar felt my remark to the press was uncalled for and that it was a tremendous criticism of him as a player. I didn't think so then, and don't now. Convinced otherwise, Edgar told me he was going to leave the team. I told him I could understand his unhappiness, but that in my opinion he would be making a great mistake to quit. Nevertheless, he did.

I left the door open for him to return, but never pursued him, and he dropped out for good. Much to my surprise, we became a better ball club almost immediately. Some say it was the loss to Houston that made us a better ball club, and some say it was the loss of Lacey. I think it was a combination of things.

From that time on, with Lynn and Shackelford at forwards and Alcindor at center, we became probably as strong a basketball team—a college team, that is—as the game has ever seen. Though not as good an outside shooter as Shackelford, Lynn was excellent as a number one on the 1–2–1–1 zone press because he was so deceptive. He was not fast, but, oh, how quick were those hands, so alert to tip the ball loose on the inbound pass.

Warren and Allen, together for the second season at guards, were a superb combination. Having Mike Warren on the floor was almost like having a coach there. He totally understood my philosophy and ran the game the way I wanted it.

With Mike in command of things, that second year of the Alcindor era—as the press called it—we improved steadily all season, from our Houston defeat in the Astrodome to our triumph over Houston in the semifinals of the NCAA Championships at the Los Angeles Sports Arena. That was the night Lynn Shackelford rose to the occasion. Assigned to Hayes as the chaser in the diamond and one, Shack did an excellent job. His sole assignment was Hayes. He was to chase him, no matter where he went. If he got the ball, Shack was to get right on top of him, try his best to keep him from shooting. Let him drive by you, I counseled him; then Lewis will take over. Our primary charge to Shack was to try and keep Hayes from ever getting the ball, to play him so tight they wouldn't pass to him. It was a tremendous individual defensive effort by a player who was not normally a good defender.

But our young men went out that night supercharged. In fact, I worried about their being too high. All remembered the Astrodome, and all remembered the comments of the Big E of what Houston was going to do to UCLA. It wasn't too good a ball game for ten minutes or so, but then the press and the diamond and one began to tell. Hayes got his first field goal at the 10:57 mark of the first half. That cut our lead to 20–19, but that was really the end. In the next five minutes—with probably the greatest blitz any of my teams has ever put together—we outscored Houston, 21-5. They were down, 41-24, with six minutes still left in the half. They got two scattered field goals in that run but, most important, they kicked the ball away eleven times in the first half, most of them during this streak.

Every one of our players was dedicated to that game. The fact that we beat North Carolina the next night for our fourth NCAA title, the second time we had two in succession, was anticlimactic, at least for the spectators. They came for the Houston affair and that's what it was. Quite an affair, and an impressive victory. One writer, I believe from the East, expressed to me later his amazement that our players didn't seem too jubilant about winning from North Carolina, 78-55.

I told him what I told my players on the bench as the clock ran down. "I don't want any out-of-control celebration. I want you to feel good, cut down the nets—but I don't want any jumping around, no dancing on the floor or acting like fools. No excessive jubilation, no spectacle." What I was really saying to them was, don't climb a mountain. And when we lose, as we did earlier that year at the Astrodome, my words of caution, "Don't hang your heads, don't bellyache, walk out with your head high," are to remind them not to descend into the lowest valley, but to climb a steadily rising plane as they strive to reach their ultimate potential.

Just give me a group of gentlemen, who play the game hard but clean, and always on an upward path. Then the championships will take care of themselves if the overall ability of the team warrants them.

23

Ability may get you to the top, but it takes character to keep you there.

BY THE TIME OF Lewis Alcindor's senior season in 1968-69, it was obvious that all the glowing forecasts about him were true. My only problem was to see that the infection of success didn't set in to spoil the team's final year.

We had already been beset with a major problem that cost us a great guard in Lucius Allen. He had become entangled with the police on a charge of possession of marijuana. It was dismissed, but within a year to the day of that charge he was hit with another. It was not generally known, however, that he had actually quit school before that happened.

It was a tremendous loss for Lucius and UCLA. I felt more concern for Lucius than for our problem because I felt his future was unlimited. It is a tribute to him that he came back from this adversity to become an established star in the NBA. He has tremendous ability, is one of the most likable young men I have ever known, but is weak in many respects. I pray that he has no further trouble.

We were going into the year again built around the low post offense tailored for Lewis. Shackelford was back, but now both Allen and Warren were gone from the back line. That's one place where I always plan for experience, but man's best plans often go astray, and this was an example.

We had plenty of power up front. Two highly talented sophomores were on hand—Curtis Rowe and Sidney Wicks—and a top back-up center, Steve Patterson, who had been held out a year. But who would run our offense was a real question mark. Kenny Heitz was back at guard, but I didn't think he was strong enough to be the lead guard and direct the attack. Our hope seemed to rest in reserve Bill Sweek and another senior who had sat out a year, Don Saffer, but there simply was no established back court general.

Coming in from Orange Coast was a new man I had seen play once as a forward. John Vallely, at 6′ 2½″, had been a high school center and later a jaycee forward. There was something about him, however—his quickness, his shooting ability, and his competitive desire—that seemed to me to spell guard. It was difficult to say why.

A year before, I had talked to Jerry Tarkanian, now coach at Cal State Long Beach but then at Pasadena City College, about Vallely. Jerry thought he could play the back court. Ironically, when we really decided we wanted Vallely, Jerry was at Long Beach and was the toughest competition we had for the boy. We were the only two schools, I believe, who were seriously interested.

Whether John could be a starter for us or even do much I didn't know, but I sure wanted to give him a try. We had to have someone. And it helped that Vallely came to Los Angeles that summer and played in a lot of pickup games at guard with Mike Warren and some of our other kids. It was a good way to get a little familiar with what we were doing.

By the time we opened the season against Purdue, I had pretty well established that Vallely would be a starting guard and run the offense. That was a tremendous decision for me to make and accept. Normally, I don't think it best to bring a new man in and give him such a task unless he is out of this world, like an Alcindor or someone of that caliber. I prefer to have a man earn his way into the top unit, but when no one has established himself, your hand is forced.

Vallely adapted rapidly. Unfortunately, just when it was time to open in the Midwest for games with Ohio State and Notre Dame, he came down with the flu and couldn't play. That set him back so far that it appeared he might not be able to come up to the challenge of starting. By the opening of the conference, however, Vallely had convinced me. He had a fine series in the Holiday Festival in Madison Square Garden, getting 31 points against St. John's in the championship game.

Now we had the floor leader we needed to complete the five for Lewis's senior season. Lewis had reached a point where it was difficult to find even a small flaw in his game. As a sophomore and junior his timing had been a little uncertain on occasion, but now it was precise. Experience with our style and general maturity had developed this finesse and all the other necessary ones to near perfection. For a player as gifted as Lewis, it would have been simple to become blasé, to take things too easily. Not Lewis. He was a competitor, always pushing himself, always pressing to become greater.

Even though he is now an established superstar in professional basketball, I am convinced that his greatest years are still to come. He has not yet attained full maturity but even when he does—and everyone then starts downhill physically—his knowledge, experience, and intelligence will carry him on a plateau for several years. Only an injury or some unforeseen circumstance can prevent him from being the most valuable player in the history of the game, if he is not already that.

One of Lewis's greatest attributes was his ability to adapt to any situation. After the so-called Alcindor rule was passed—the outlawing of the dunk shot—some skeptics said he wouldn't be as great. They ignored his tremendous desire and determination. He worked twice as hard on banking shots off the glass, his little hook across the lane, and his turnaround jumper.

We were 29 and 1 again his senior year—88 wins

and 2 defeats in three years—and while we had some fine talent to team with him, I do not believe we would have established that kind of a record without Alcindor.

That lone loss his senior year was our first ever in Pauley Pavilion. It came at the hands of USC. That year we closed the Pacific Eight season with back-to-back games—Friday and Saturday—against the Trojans at the Sports Arena and Pauley. It was probably as great a two-game series as those two rivals ever played—or any two teams, for that matter.

We won Friday night in a double overtime, 61-55, and were lucky to do it. USC seemed to have the game won in the first overtime, 47-45, with just four seconds to play. I am sure USC expected the ball to go to Lewis but two quick passes found it in Shackelford's hands. Deep in the left corner, twenty-five or thirty feet away, Shack jumped and popped. As the buzzer went off, the shot dropped through for another tie. It was Lynn's first shot of the game, but probably one of the most dramatic he ever took. We came back in the second overtime to put the Trojans away. Once more, I felt that superior condition and confidence turned things around.

Bob Boyd's deliberate, slow-paced attack against us had been very effective. On the next night at Pauley he used the same tactics, and again it was a classic intracity battle. Lewis tied things up at 44 all with 1:15 to play. USC, as it had all night, worked deliberately, moving carefully as they tried to find an opening. With 19 seconds remaining, Bob Boyd called time for his Trojans. As the clock began to tick, USC worked cautiously, until finally Don Crenshaw set a screen and Ernie Powell jumped up to pop one in. We had seconds to go as we came down court for one shot, but this time Shackelford was not free. Then when Sidney Wicks's 20-footer with a second to play hit the iron and bounced away, USC won, 46-44.

Much as I hate to lose, especially to USC, this defeat was beneficial. We went into the NCAA regionals in

Pauley and had little trouble in beating New Mexico, 53-38, in another slowdown game, and Santa Clara, 90-52, in a racehorse game.

Next stop was Louisville. If we could put it all together we would have an unprecedented third straight NCAA championship in the Alcindor years. We drew Drake in the first round. They were a fine club but I really didn't foresee the trouble we were to have. We might have lost if it hadn't been for John Vallely's timely baskets. As it was, John fouled out and so did Kenny Heitz.

That's the night I had a little trouble with Bill Sweek, who had played the sixth man role quite ably all year. Toward the end of the game with Vallely out and Heitz in foul trouble, I had switched Lynn Shackelford back to guard. Bill thought he should be in the game instead. Finally, when I called him to go in, he sauntered up at a rather lackadaisical pace that irritated me. I told him if he didn't care to play any more than that to go back and sit down. Well, he went back all right, but instead of to the bench to sit down, he went to the dressing room.

Now I was irate. But we still had a game that wasn't won. Shack was not a guard and with Sidney Wicks inbounding the ball, we managed to blow a six or eight point lead. We finally hit two free throws to win, 85-82, but I was so upset over Sweek's leaving the floor that it was difficult to maintain my composure.

We had a real set-to in the dressing room. I almost went in the shower after Bill. I was very disappointed at his attitude for not wanting to go in when he was needed. We went round and round, but while I may flare up—as I did that night—I try never to hold a grudge. Bill was in there when we won against Purdue, 92-72, in the championship the next night, hitting three for three from the floor and providing that extra spark so vital in the sixth man role.

I know how a boy feels in such a situation. I know how I felt when I was in grammar school in Centerton and Earl Warriner didn't play me. It's a tough situation for a competitor, and Bill Sweek was a competitor.

Shortly after that, Bill asked me to write a letter of recommendation for him to get into the Peace Corps or the ministry, and I was glad to comply. He chose the Peace Corps.

It's when you have boys like Sweek, who'll fight you as hard as the opponent, and boys like Alcindor, whose talent is so great it's hard to appreciate, that you reflect back over your career and thank the Lord for allowing you to be the coach of such fine young men.

24

I will get ready and then, perhaps, my chance will come.

WITH THE GRADUATION of Lewis Alcindor, Kenny Heitz, Lynn Shackelford, and Co., a tremendous era in UCLA basketball ended. Many people believed that I would regret the departure of such a dominant force. I did, just as every year I regret losing any of my boys to graduation regardless of whether they might be number one or number fifteen.

Coaches become extremely attached to their players and to their managers. Because they work with these students under conditions of severe emotional and mental stress, as well as physical, it is understandable that they establish closer relationships with them than are usual in the normal classroom situation.

While three brilliant seasons were now history, for the first time in 1095 days—three years—I could look forward to one thing. "It'll be nice to know," I told the news media, "that I'll again be doing my best to win rather than to keep from losing."

Throughout the Alcindor era, from day one, there was not, in the eyes of the public, a question of winning, but of not losing. Now I could revert to a more normal program. In 1969–70, since we had a fine, but not unusually tall, post man in Steve Patterson, that meant going back to my regular high post office. While Steve was not a superstar of the Alcindor style, he was nonetheless a talent any coach would be pleased to have. He was a good blocker and screener, and in his way, a rather impressive feeder to men cutting through to the basket. His ability to shoot from the key made our high post offense more effective.

With Patterson on the post we could present probably the most powerful front line, from a purely physical point of view, that I had ever had. Steve was 6' 9" and weighed 221. Curtis Rowe, who started virtually all the way as a sophomore, was on one side. He was 6' 6½" and 216. A certain coming star, Sidney Wicks, at 6' 8" and 220, would be at the other forward. Although as a sophomore he had some trouble fitting into my style of play, I was confident that he was to become a superplayer. He was the quickest and fastest big man I had ever coached. That gave us real power, and tremendous board strength at either end of the floor. The quickness present in those three men would surprise a lot of people.

Our back court situation looked good. John Vallely, who had made such tremendous strides in the transition from a junior college forward to UCLA guard, was back for his final year. As the floor leader, he ran the show, but now he had a real hand running with him in Henry Bibby, a 6' 1" sophomore from Franklinton, North Carolina. Henry had been an impressive shooter on our freshman team and I looked forward to three years of such shooting with the varsity.

Regardless of what is expected of a new season, there are certain rituals to liven up the early weeks. One of my annual little stands comes in mid-October. Although it varies a bit each time I write it, my fall letter tells my prospective players almost the same thing every year. "You must report for practice with no beards, no goatees, no mustaches. Sideburns can be no longer than the beginning of the lobes of the ear and the hair must be a reasonable length. I will be the sole judge of what is reasonable." This policy is again made clear at the meeting I have about two weeks before practice starts.

No matter what my letter says, occasionally some

player or players will test me. Under the rules, organized practice cannot be held until October 15, but press and picture day may be scheduled one day earlier. One year, and I won't say what year, one of our stars came with extra long sideburns, one with a goatee, and another with mutton chops to draw their game equipment. Always on hand for this, I just stopped them, looked at my watch, and said: "You have twenty minutes to decide whether you're going to play basketball at UCLA this year or not. There are clippers and razors in the training room."

"You'll be crucified," one of them said.

"That may well be, but you won't be around to see it."

They decided in a hurry. Well within the allotted time they were back and passed inspection. Later they kidded me about it occasionally, and all of them at one time or another tried to find out what they'd been afraid to test me on earlier. "You really wouldn't have stuck to it, would you, coach?"

"You'll never really know, will you?" My reply still didn't commit me. "I'm the only one who really knows that."

Once during the summer when his hair was quite long, another very prominent player asked me, "What would you do if I refused to have my hair cut?"

"I won't do anything."

"I thought you wouldn't let us wear our hair real long."

"I won't. It's quite all right; you can wear your hair any way you want. I can't determine how long you wear your hair. All I can determine is whether or not you play."

"I thought there was a catch," he said, as my words sank in.

"That's right."

Thus far I have stood firm on the haircut issue. In other areas involving appearance I have relented some. One needs only to talk to any player of five, six or ten years ago to find that out. I am flexible to a point and that point I establish from year to year.

It's just like our style of play. Basically, I haven't changed from a fast-break, pressure defense since my first day at Dayton High. But anyone who can objectively evaluate my teams over all those years can see the changes made necessary by the talent, the rules revisions, and the tremendous increase in the physique and the physical skills of the athletes.

The 1969-70 team was a striking example of that last factor. How many times in history has one team had a front line with such power as we did? You don't often put together three physical specimens like Wicks, Rowe, and Patterson. Furthermore, John Ecker, the first front-line replacement and a fine young man, was also of their size. They looked more like tight end candidates for the Los Angeles Rams than front-line men for a college basketball team. Even the two guards, Bibby and Vallely, were big for guards on my team. Surprisingly often, I have had one outstanding guard on a team who would be 6 feet or under, such as Eddie Sheldrake, Ron Livingston, Mike Warren, and others.

Bibby is an example of how much a team means to the individual man. As a sophomore with John Vallely, Bibby was third in scoring with 468 points and a 15.6 average while shooting 50.1 percent from the floor. That year it was Vallely's responsibility to bring the ball down court, direct the offense, and handle the ball in most of the pressure situations. Seldom had a sophomore guard shot so well from outside as did Bibby. He probably had more leeway from me as to how far out he could shoot from than any first year man I ever coached. His success was excellent.

The next two years, with Vallely gone, the whole burden of bringing down the ball, directing the attack, and handling the pressure situations was Henry's. He never shot as well again. He began to force his shots and failed to concentrate as much on the act of shooting.

Perhaps I was remiss in giving Henry so much freedom but I kept thinking that he would come back to his form of that sophomore season and I never wanted to hurt his confidence. In all other respects, Henry Bibby became one of the great guards in the country, tough on defense, sure of himself, confident in our concept and ultimately one of the many outstanding guards I have had in my coaching career.

My goal every year is to make basketball a pleasure, not a poison. This year, 1969-70, was one of the real fun years I have enjoyed in coaching. We had a unique bunch of players. Most of the team had basked in the fame of Lewis's senior season. Some of them, like Rowe and Vallely, had achieved a certain amount of personal acclaim as well, but basically, UCLA was an unknown quantity.

One of the big ifs was that awesome looking young man, Sidney Wicks. As a sophomore, Sidney had disappointed me almost as often as he had made me happy. Feeling that he didn't have his game under control, I didn't start him many times that year. He was still too much of an individual to work into my concept of team play. Sidney, of course, did not like the fact that he wasn't starting all of the time when he knew he was physically better than others.

That year, Rowe played 912 minutes, Shackelford 469, and Sidney 473. Rowe, who was also a sophomore on the final Alcindor team, played almost twice as much as Sidney who had physical equipment and greater individual talent. But Curtis was also talented and was, perhaps, the most consistent three-year starting forward that I have ever coached. He didn't have bad games; some were just better than others.

When I wrote my annual letter to the team on July 7, 1970, it was pointed probably more to Sidney Wicks than I realized at the time. I must emphasize, however, that Sidney was never selfish. Quite the contrary, he was always a fine team player, but his individual style did not fit in at first, and tended to make his play and our team play somewhat inconsistent.

"In group activity," I wrote, "there must be supervision and leadership and a disciplined effort by all, or much of our united strength will be dissipated pulling against ourselves.

"If you discipline yourself toward team effort under the supervision of the one in charge, even though you might not always agree with the decisions, much can and will be accomplished.

"Your lot is certain failure without discipline.

"I am very interested in each of you as an individual but I must act in what I consider to be in the best interest of the team for either the moment or the future.

"Your race or your religion will have no bearing on my judgment, but your ability and how it works to my philosophy of team play very definitely will. Furthermore, your personal conduct and adherence to standards that I make will undoubtedly be taken into consideration either consciously or unconsciously.

"There may seem to be double standards at times as I most certainly will not treat you all alike in every respect. However, I will attempt to give each individual the treatment he earns and deserves according to my judgment, in keeping with what I consider in the best interest of the team. You must accept this in the proper manner for you to be a positive and contributing member ..."

It had been difficult for Sidney as a sophomore to fit into the wing style of play that was necessary with Lewis on the deep post. Sidney wanted to drive the basket, but with Lewis deep underneath and the defense always sagging in on him, there was no place for Sidney to drive. He reached on defense, he tried to steal too often, he slashed in on the board to grab the spectacular rebound; but being out of control he would often come down and foul an opponent or miss out on a rebound he should have had.

It was difficult, too, for him to see Lynn Shackelford pop them in from deep in the corner—twenty, twenty-five, and, rarely, thirty feet out. Sidney felt he should be allowed to shoot from farther than the eighteen-foot halter I had put on him. One day during his senior year, after I had jumped him pretty hard in a game for taking low percentage shots, for him—out beyond eighteen feet—he asked:

"If I can hit ten in a row from here," he said, pointing to an imaginary line about twenty-five feet out and at a little more of an angle than I preferred, "will you let me shoot from here in a game?"

"I sure will." This was well out on the side in an area that I consider to be the most difficult, lowest percentage shot in basketball, because you can't use the board and the angle is bad.

Sidney, I guess, didn't believe what he had heard.

"If I get ten in a row, can I?"

"Sure, Sidney, if you get ten in a row, I'll let you shoot from there."

Do you know, that determined competitor got out there and hit nine in succession, nine low percentage shots, before he missed?

"That ought to be good enough, huh, coach?" Sidney asked.

"Not for me. You won't do that when somebody is snapping his hand in your face." Sidney just laughed and went on to the next phase of warm-up. He knew deep down I was right, that he had a run of good fortune and that the odds were too much against him to take another try, but he was very pleased at what he had showed me. What he did not know was that I was equally pleased.

The 1969–70 team won the conference, although we lost two games, one to Oregon, 78–65, and the other to USC, 87–86, the latter only our second loss at Pauley. We ended up with a 28 and 2 season and a fourth successive NCAA title, two more than anyone else had ever been able to win.

And that power line of Sidney, Curtis, and Steve was something else. When I automatically put Sidney in opposite Curtis, he arrived. Not immediately, but dramatically, as the season progressed. Now our style was cut for a power driver like him. With Patterson working off a high post, both Wicks and Rowe could effectively cut and drive.

Those three had quite a year. Wicks led us in scoring with an 18.6 average, Rowe had 15.3 and Patterson 12.5 That was an average of 15.4 for the front line.

But I feel the team really came together in defeat. Once more this appeared to be the catalyst. USC had whipped us by a point in another wild battle at Pauley and again we were to close out the season on Saturday night with the Trojans in the Sports Arena. I never want to lose to the Trojans and never back-to-back games, but especially not the week before the NCAA playoffs. This subconsciously gets to the players, I feel, hurting their morale and bothering their tempo.

This night was not Sidney Wicks's night. From the start, he was miserable. Everything he did was wrong and every time he made an error, USC seemed to capitalize on it. When I took him out, we had a nose-to-nose confrontation right there on the Arena floor. I finally told him to go down to the end of the bench and stay there until he felt he was ready to play.

After about five minutes he came stalking down to me, looking like he was going to eat me alive, and announced he was ready to play. I let him sit another couple of minutes. In the next four and a half minutes, plus about seventeen minutes or so in the second half, Sidney played the greatest basketball he ever played. He had 16 rebounds and was 9 for 11 from the field and 13 for 18 from the free throw line for a total of 31 points.

This moment, coupled with his tremendous display in the NCAA championship game against Artis Gilmore of Jacksonville where he literally destroyed this great 7 footer, turned Sidney Wicks around from an erratic, great player into a superplayer.

Sidney was a skilled talent. But once again my belief was substantiated that a youngster must practice self-discipline and get his game under team control if he is to reach individual stardom and the team success. Sidney certainly did that rather dramatically in his junior year, and no one was more pleased or happier for him than his coach. Sidney still feels that he should have started as a sophomore, and I do, too. I also believe that I was right in not starting him then and that Sidney was the one that prevented it, not his coach.

25

The main ingredient of stardom is the rest of the team.

ONCE AGAIN IN 1970–71, we were picked to win the NCAA. We had now won six in the past seven years—four in a row—and if one was to believe the experts in the news media, all we had to do to add another was to show up for thirty consecutive games.

We were going to be tough, there was no doubt about that. We had four starters back from the sixth NCAA champions—Wicks, Rowe, Patterson, and Bibby—but we were faced with the problem of trying to come up with a floor leader. We needed a replacement for the graduated John Vallely, who had been dubbed "Money Man" by his teammates because of his clutch shooting.

Before the season began, I warned the returning starters of the pitfalls and problems we would encounter. An impressive lot of seniors, they might tend to become intolerable, and I was going to be sure that didn't take place.

We didn't have that able ball-handling guard that I could foresee, which meant we had to go with our strength, our power line. Our immediate problem at the outset of practice was to determine who would be the starting guard alongside Henry Bibby. There was no real standout. But in the weeks between the opening of practice in mid-October and our first game with Baylor, I had narrowed it down to one of two men, Kenny

Booker and Terry Schofield. Both were seniors, and in spelling Bibby and Vallely both had logged considerable playing time the year before. The final selection was difficult and required careful analysis.

Schofield, the better shooter of the two, had come to UCLA from Santa Monica City College. Beaten out of an expected starting role when Vallely came in from junior college to earn it with no prior exposure to our style and system, Terry had been an unhappy youngster the past two years.

Now I decided that Terry still wouldn't be a starter—that I would go with Booker, who was just an inch taller at 6' 4", but who played just a little better defense and worked in more smoothly with the others. Our new starting five of Wicks, Rowe, Patterson, Bibby, and Booker averaged just a shade under 6' 5½"—the tallest and heaviest starting team I had ever coached.

Before announcing the decision between Booker and Schofield, I talked to Terry about it, pointing out that he was the sixth man, that he was probably going to play as much as, perhaps even more than, Booker, and that he was vital to our hopes. The team needed not only his outside shooting but his ability to come off the bench and inject that propulsive spark and drive that would get us untracked. Terry accepted that analysis and had a fine year for himself and the team.

I had feared that an irreparable gap might come between us over that decision. But it didn't. Terry Schofield played the role of the sixth man to the hilt, doing a tremendous job for us. Later he told me that he "grew up that year." Seeing him arrive as a basketball player and as a young man is the sort of gratification that makes a coach happy. All the effort is suddenly worth it because Terry Schofield, like so many others who have crossed my path in all these years, has found his place in the sun.

It is difficult sometimes to reach a team that is so weighted with experience. Most of them had been on two national championship teams and had already been labeled by sportswriters and sportscasters for a third. These were big, strong, experienced players who knew they were big, strong, and experienced players. It was difficult to keep them from becoming complacent. My hardest job all year was to fight the "I-can-get-the-job-done-when-I-turn-it-on" attitude and to keep them striving to improve.

It was difficult, too, to keep their minds on the problem at hand when the world, especially the pro basketball world, came knocking at their door. I never saw any more mail under the names of the various pro clubs than arrived for Wicks, Rowe, and Patterson. When we were flying to Houston for the NCAA finals in the Astrodome, Sidney was sitting directly in front of me and Mrs. Wooden. He had a cassette player with him, and I'll never forget the song he was listening to. "If I Were a Rich Man"—something like that. I reached over and tapped him on the shoulder.

"Sidney," I said, "I wish I had your opportunities to be a millionaire."

There was no player aboard who had gone to Houston with us in the Alcindor years when we lost that mid-season affair in the Astrodome. All of them, though, had either seen the game on television or had read and heard about it. They were quietly determined to change our record in that "Eighth Wonder of the World" arena—which definitely is not the best place in the world for the basketball fan.

We had had a good year in 1970–71, losing only once, to Notre Dame in South Bend, 89–82. Although it was not one of our better games, Notre Dame had a fine ball club. Led by the great Austin Carr, they purely and simply outplayed us and richly deserved their victory.

We had several other struggles that year. One was a 64–60 win at USC in which we had to come from behind, but we beat them quite easily in Pauley Pavilion later on. Instead of playing these games on consecutive nights as we had been doing recently, one took place about mid-season and the other was the final conference affair.

We had two extremely tight games in Oregon. On a Friday we barely beat Oregon at Eugene, 69–68. A late steal by Henry Bibby was the key play. The next night, we went down to the wire with Oregon State before we could win, 67–65, and this time it was Sidney Wicks who won it. After getting well behind in the early going, we had to labor through that whole game.

Eventually we tied it up, and in the closing minutes, with the ball in our possession, we were playing out the time for Sidney to drive by the big man guarding him. He was playing Sidney a little loose, giving him the outside in order to protect the drive where Sidney might either get the basket, the foul, or both. Finally Sidney got just a bit of an edge, faked the drive to freeze his man, then put up a jump shot from just outside the circle. It dropped through the loop just about as time ran out.

One thing that I have learned over the years in which we have been so fortunate in NCAA championship play is not to work the team too hard once we have the conference won and are certain of going into the playoffs. We keep them in top shape but without too much contact. We do a lot of group work—two on two, three on three, etc.—to keep up the momentum and the unity. I also build confidence. I point out to them that they got this far with what they have been doing and now is no time to change. We play our game and try not to permit an opponent to force us into theirs.

One of basketball's prime tenents is discipline. You must maintain it. Most of my players who have gone into professional basketball come back to tell me how valuable the discipline they learned at UCLA has been in the pro leagues.

There is no replacement for sound fundamentals and strict discipline. They will reinforce you in the toughest circumstance. The importance of little things cannot be overemphasized—like double-tying the shoestrings; seeing that uniforms and shoes are properly fitted; and forming the habit, based on the assumption that every shot will be missed, of getting your hands above your shoulders when a shot is taken so you can come down with the rebound.

I've heard coaches say that you can't do much with a player's shooting ability, his speed, his quickness, or the height he can jump. I agree to a certain extent, but I also believe you can improve those skills.

At the 1964 Olympic basketball team trials a study was made by Joe Brown, a trainer with the physical education department at the University of Kentucky. Six members of our first NCAA champions were trying out for the Olympic team—Kenny Washington, Keith Erickson, Fred Slaughter, Gail Goodrich, Jack Hirsch and Doug McIntosh. (Hazzard did not participate in the test.) All candidates were given what is called the sergeant jump and reaction test. This is a vertical jump test where each player stands sideways to a wall with his feet together and the arm next to the wall extended upward as high as he can reach without rising on his toes. An observer indicates that spot with a chalk mark. Next the player squats and jumps as high as he can. The observer again marks the extent of the player's reach. The jump is repeated three times and the score based on the difference in inches between the first mark and the highest mark corrected to the lowest number.

Washington and Erickson tied for first with a 36 score. Slaughter was third at 30: Goodrich—probably the smallest man—was fourth at 29. Jack Hirsch tied Dave Stallworth at 28 and McIntosh was at 27 with the likes of Rick Barry, Jeff Mullins, Bill Bradley, "Cotton" Nash, "Bad News" Barnes, Jerry Sloan, and "Butch' Komives.

"UCLA's success in overpowering these [taller teams from Duke and Michigan] for the national championship," Brown pointed out in his report, "can be attributed to many factors; but, in this author's opinion, a very important contributing factor may have been the great jumping ability of the UCLA players."

He also concluded that "UCLA's work index is 8 percent greater than the NCAA Olympians, 10 percent greater than the NCAA alternates and 12 percent greater than the NCAA Olympic trials participants."

He concluded that "a basketball team with players who can jump with power and efficiency, regardless of physical height and weight, will generally have a much better chance to win the important games on its schedule."

We continually drill on jumping, rebounding, and timing. Thus, when we get a big club like the 1970–71 team with that power line of Wicks, Rowe, and Patterson, we are tough on the boards for balls that go up in a scramble. Once again, every drill has its purpose. Not only are they devised to improve general condition, but also improve some basic fundamental of the game.

The proper execution of fundamentals can become instinctive if taught properly, just like breathing or walking. The crucial factor in basketball is that most of them must be done at full speed, running. When they become instinctive under these circumstances, you're tough. That's what became second nature to most of the NCAA champions.

Such instinctive control was very visible in the power line during our final two games in the Astrodome. We beat Kansas in the NCAA semifinals, 68–60, and then had a real set-to with Villanova in the finals. When it was all over, we had a six-point edge, 68–62. (I'm still not too proud to settle for one more than our opponents. Sidney Wicks, incidentally, played with a very sore foot in the championship game and, although not up to par, made some very key plays.

One of the most gratifying moments in my entire coaching career came afterwards in the Astrodome as I walked in our dressing room door. I heard some writer ask Curtis Rowe, "What kind of racial problems did you have on the UCLA team?"

Curtis, without hesitation, looked at him in that firm, strong way of his, and said, "Coach Wooden doesn't see color."

Then he turned and went into the shower.

26

Young people need models, not critics.

"It has been a long time since I have looked forward so eagerly to a coming basketball season and I hope that you share this enthusiasm."

That was the opening sentence in my annual letter to the squad on July 28, 1971. It was a most sincere and forthright declaration. Even though that power line of Wicks, Row, and Patterson was gone and only one starter, Henry Bibby, was back, I was eager to get going. I felt that the squad epitomized the saying "Youth must be served."

I wrote: "The 1971–72 Bruins will be short on experience in comparison with most of our recent teams, but it will not be short on talent, and I would much rather have talent without experience than experience without talent."

There was talent. It was led by another big man who some claimed was of the Alcindor caliber but from a different mold. Bill Walton, an angular redhead from San Diego who stood 6' 11", had potential defensive skills that might be compared to those of the fabled Bill Russell. There were two excellent sophomore guards in Greg Lee, whose father played at UCLA prior to my arrival in 1948, and Tommy Curtis, a quick, but smaller sophomore from Tallahassee, Florida. A strong contender at forward was Keith Wilkes, a 6' 6" sophomore from Santa Barbara, who was only a few months past his eighteenth birthday when practice commenced October 15.

There were two junior forwards who had played well in relief to the power line the year before. One was Larry Hollyfield, a 6' 5" all-everything from Compton. He probably possessed as good a one-on-one talent as anyone out but had problems adapting to the system. Larry Farmer from Denver, Colorado, also 6' 5", was a steady cornerman with good rebounding talent.

There were others—Gary Franklin, a 6' 5" sophomore forward; 6' 5½" Vince Carson, who had been hurt his senior season at John Muir High in Pasadena; Swen Nater, a 6' 11" center, who had transferred from Cypress Junior College and had sat out a year. Swen was born in Holland and had played only two years of basketball.

To bind all this youthful skill together, we had Henry Bibby, now a senior and twice a key back-court man on NCAA champions. A tireless worker who fully understood our philosophy, he gave our team the assurance, security, and leadership so vitally essential to its eventual success.

This was the talent. On paper, and based on the freshman season, they had fine potential. I was convinced that if everything would fall in place, if the players would accept all our precepts of play, conduct, condition, discipline, team welfare, and avoid any individual personality clashes, it could be a "very rewarding year."

How did I forecast the season in my little envelope locked in the top drawer of my desk? I foresaw 24 wins, 2 defeats.

I feared we would probably lose to Oregon State in Corvallis early in January. They loomed as very strong, and it would be the first road game for our extremely young team. Fortunately, we would have time to build our confidence in a pre-conference schedule of eight games all to be played on our home court—Pauley Pavilion. Although I was worried about our conference opener, I anticipated we would have the Pacific Eight

Conference won going into the final regularly scheduled game with USC at the Sports Arena. I figured we would lose that one because I expected to be concentrating that week on preparations for the NCAA regionals at Provo, Utah.

I told no one, of course, except my wife, of my prediction.

One of the attributes of the 1971–72 teams—which our sportswriter friends tagged the Walton Gang or Bibby's Bunch—was its intelligence. Not only basketball intelligence—the players as a whole probably had more academic brilliance than any team I have ever had. Walton, Wilkes, and Greg Lee were all fine students; and Farmer and Bibby, the other two starters, were good students—not brilliant but good.

It was an easy team with which to work. With the big man once more in Bill Walton, I went back to a set offense similar to the one I had used with Lewis. Our players' balance around the big man and the fact that they got along so well as a team was important in getting it all together.

Once more we had someone other than a guard to lead us on the floor. Just as Sidney Wicks in his senior year had taken command of both ends of the court, Bill Walton now came forward. Visibly happy playing basketball and all-seeing on the court, this gifted young man talked more during a game and called out more warnings and advice to his teammates than any player I have ever had.

Every expert sees something else of great import in Walton's talent. In my mind, next to tremendous ability and unselfish team play, his foremost offensive skill was on the outlet pass. Never have I coached a player who was more skilled at outletting the ball to initiate a fast break. He always had the ball ready to throw even before he came down with the rebound. In fact, there were times when the ball was nearly at mid-court before Bill's feet hit the floor. On defense his intimidating shot-blocking was his greatest asset.

With no great speed in the guards to compare with

what we had had in the years with Walt Hazzard or Mike Warren or earlier with Eddie Sheldrake, we still capitalized on the break. Once that was stopped, however, we had a strong set offense with Walton underneath, Bibby on the left wing where he was a definite shooting threat, and Farmer on the right wing. In this offense, Larry, a strong rebounder, was vital on the side away from both the big post man and most effective outside shooter. Pencil-thin Keith Wilkes, a good passer and feeder, was excellent coming up from the low to the high post. Not nearly as strong as Curtis Rowe, Wilkes was equally adept at doing a job that few recognized, and he seemed to have been born just as consistent. Seldom did he have a bad game. If his shooting was off, his defense, rebounding, and general play contributed greatly.

Once again, I was confronted with a difficult problem in determining how to place the fifth and sixth men—sophomores Greg Lee and Tommy Curtis. Each had attributes the other didn't. Going down to the wire again, I finally selected Greg. He was taller and bigger, and a little headier on what to do. And since he got the ball into the high post a little better than Tommy. I felt he would complement Walton more.

On the other hand, Curtis was quicker and stronger on the pressing defense, but the thing that clinched my decision was Tommy's ability coming off the bench. I felt he would be far more valuable coming in as that sixth man than starting every time as the fifth. Yet the one game when Greg couldn't play because of an injury the night before, Curtis started, played a tremendous game, scored 14 points, and did everything one could possibly ask of a starter. Furthermore, it was against Ohio State, our most respected and capable opponent up to that date.

Tommy showed what a fine young man he was when in the very next game I started Greg again. I know that was a bitter pill for Tommy, but he never brooded about it. Convinced that Greg could never give us that dynamic thrust we needed from time to time out of the sixth man, I had to hold Tommy in readiness for those crucial moments. There was many a time in winning those 30 games in 1971–72 without a single defeat that his teammates turned to Curtis. "Come on, Tommy," I've heard them say during a time-out or a brief break, "liven us up. Get us going."

By the time we went on our first road trip to Oregon State in January, I was convinced that we had a superclub. Just how super a club so young could be over a full season was yet to be demonstrated. But it had really matured in those eight games at home without defeat. We had averaged 108 points, including our 79–53 win over Ohio State in the finals of the Bruin Classic, while our opponents averaged only 63 points. It was now obvious that not only were we a pretty strong offensive force despite our youth and inexperience, but exceptionally tough defensively.

Many pointed to the big man, Walton, as the reason for the defensive strength, and it was obvious that he was a major contributor. But everyone else was tough on defense, too. With Bill directing things vocally, they played it tight and we didn't get burned too often.

Youth must mature with experience, but this squad matured with more rapidity than I had any right to expect. It certainly must have been the youngest team in average age to go through a season undefeated and win the NCAA. It was a delightful team with which to work, with a minimum of problems and a maximum of success. The never-ceasing hustle of Henry Bibby, our only returning starter from the year before, in each and every practice was an inspiration to the younger players.

Not an overly emotional group, they let their play speak for them. Most of the boys would probably agree that our victory against Cal State Long Beach in the regionals at Provo, Utah, was the most satisfactory moment in a perfect season, but our toughest game was in the NCAA finals against Florida State at the Los Angeles Sports Arena.

We were never in danger of losing a ball game, as

far as score was concerned late in a game. The NCAA record we set for average margin of victory over the season attests to that fact. In thirty victories we averaged 94.6 points against 64.3 points for our opponents, or a difference of 30.3 points per game. This was accomplished with no player averaging over thirty-one minutes of playing time per game. Bibby and Walton had the most, averaging just under thirty-one minutes per game.

It was a fine team. We got great play all year from the starting five—Wilkes, Farmer, Walton, Lee, and Bibby—plus some brilliant service from Curtis. Swen Nater, Larry Hollyfield, and the others.

Every game, I was asked the obvious. Who was the better big man, Alcindor or Walton? I never make comparisons, even of which is the best team I have coached or which is the best player. Even after the statistical comparison was made between Lewis's sophomore season and Bill's sophomore season, I refused. Lewis averaged 29.1 points, Bill 21.1. They were even in rebounds, 466 in 30 games for 15.5 average. Lewis hit 346 of 519 shots for 66.7 percent and Bill hit 238 of 372 for 62.9 percent. Bill hit 157 of 223 free throws for 70.4 percent and Lewis hit 178 of 274 for 64.9 percent.

One conclusion is obvious. They both were very talented, both were excellent team men, both were very unselfish, and both were superb defensive men. But my comment when I was first asked to compare them after our first 1971–72 win, was the same as after our NCAA championship, and it will always be the same:

"I was most happy and pleased with Lewis for three years and I have been most happy and pleased with Bill for his years."

27

When we are out of sympathy with the young, then our work in this world is over.

ON AUGUST 1, 1972, I sat down to pen my annual letter to the squad. My profession is truly a pleasure, I reflected, as I thought about the continuing inspiration I have received from the many young men who have played for me. The group I was addressing myself to had gone 30–0 the year before, and the great majority were now only juniors.

"It is my sincere hope," I wrote to each, "that the 1972–73 UCLA varsity basketball team will be made up of players who love a challenge. Not only will there be a real battle for the top seven or eight playing spots, but the team pressure from the press and public will be far more severe than last year because now you will be expected to win.

"Many of you are partially responsible for this enviable, or unenviable, position as far as team pressure is concerned because of what you have accomplished in the past. I choose to consider it an enviable position that has been earned and that is a mark of respect. Furthermore, if you are the competitors that I think you are, you will justify the position.

"I must caution you that you cannot live in the past. The 1971–72 season is now history and we must look toward the future. The past cannot change what is to come. The work that you do each and every day is the only true way to improve and prepare yourself for what is to come. You cannot change the past and you can influence the future only by what you do today."

Shortly before we opened the season against Wisconsin, I performed another annual ritual I had begun several years earlier. Weighing carefully all the factors that would affect our upcoming season, I wrote a little message to myself, placed it in an envelope, and locked it in my desk drawer.

I devoted considerable thought to what I had said to my team back in April 1972 after our perfect season. I had complimented them, of course, telling them what a fine group of young men they were and what a pleasure it had been to work with them. But I had also added a word of caution.

"You've won a championship. You've gone through an entire season undefeated. Next year most of you will be juniors. You'll not be nearly as easy to work with because, after accomplishing the feat you have, you're going to 'feel your oats.' You won't be listening quite so well or working quite so hard. You may want to give just as much, but, subconsciously, I don't think you'll do it."

I couldn't resist adding a parting remark:

"And by the time you're seniors," I prophesied, "you'll probably be intolerable."

My prediction for each year never goes beyond our regular season. Any team that gets that far is capable of eliminating any other in the "sudden-death, one-loss-and-you're-out" NCAA championship tournament.

Once again we were in a position of trying to prevent a defeat rather than win. Although we were lacking a little in outside shooting because of the loss of Henry Bibby, that would be offset by a year's experience and greater maturity overall. And the tremendous skills Bill Walton showed as a sophomore should be even greater.

There was one last question mark in my mind before I wrote down my forecast of our season's record. That was the final game with USC. I figured we'd have the conference won by then and there might be a letdown. Furthermore, I knew that if we did have it won, I'd be preparing for the playoffs and this could be all that such a prospectively fine team would need. Nevertheless, I picked us to win them all, 26-0.

There is always concern at the beginning of a new season. Little did I know the amount that would arise very shortly, December 11, to be exact. During the wee hours on that Monday, I awoke with a severe pain in my chest. Not wanting to admit what might be happening to me, I tried to tough it out. But finally I woke Nellie, and at 1:45 a.m. was admitted to St. John's Hospital in Santa Monica.

Now, I wasn't worried about our pressing defense or our post play—only about how long a mild heart problem would keep me away from my team. For the first time in thirty-eight years, I missed a game. When we went against the University of California at Santa Barbara, my assistant, Gary Cunningham, directed the team's play while, from my hospital bed, I impatiently awaited news of the outcome. That was the only game I missed.

One special experience following my eight-day hospital stay served to remind me again what a wonderful profession I am in. Nellie had gone to the store, so I was at home alone when the doorbell rang. When I opened the door, there stood that big, lovable redhead, Bill Walton. He had come from the campus to the house on his bike just to see me in person. You know, that perked me up about as much as anything could have.

There is a lot of disparaging talk about the young these days—how callous they are, what little regard they have for their elders. But to know this young man had ridden his bike more than ten miles to visit an old gaffer who is on him all the time made me realize how false such generalities are.

Bill and his teammates were a fine group. They never failed to do what was necessary. The end was another perfect season, another NCAA title, and, more important, another season of fond memories.

How can I ever forget the magnificent performance of Walton in the championship final against Memphis

State? The inspiration and effective play of Tommy Curtis in many games, especially in the NCAA tournament against USF and Indiana? The smooth, polished brilliance Keith Wilkes displayed game after game? The solid, all-around performance of Larry Farmer? The startling steals and vibrant play of Larry Hollyfield?

Or those beautiful lob passes of Greg Lee to Walton and Farmer, especially against Memphis State? The vast improvement and productive play of David Meyers and the good humor and the fine touch provided by Swen Nater? Then, of course, there was the unpublicized but tireless dedication of those who didn't play as much but helped prepare those who did—Vince Carson, Casey Corliss, Ralph Drollinger, Gary Franklin, Pete Trgovich, and Bobby Webb.

Each year I feel I'm blessed with a remarkable group of young men. Gifted as these players are from the standpoint of basketball talent, we also want them to have the ability to get along with others, especially their teammates. This 1972–73 team had that to a remarkable degree. Their closeness, coupled with their high intelligence, stood them in good stead as we approached the University of San Francisco's all-time consecutive win record of sixty. Only the two crucial games —number 60 to tie and number 61 to break the tie— seemed to betray added strain. Once past that milestone, we could all relax. In my opinion, in fact, every game we played was in hand before we reached its last few minutes.

During the season someone asked me what would have happened if Walton had been hurt and forced to remain out. My instant answer was, "We'd win with Swen." I had great confidence in this group as team basketball players. Whether or not we could have won without Walton no one can know, of course. Naturally, our play would have been a little different with Nater, but I firmly believe we still could have won.

This was a responsive crew who always answered a challenge, no matter what it might be. I remember the Sunday before the finals against Memphis State on

Monday night. I was concerned at how taut they all seemed—perhaps even nervous. In the semifinals against Indiana we had lost our composure a bit as Indiana staged a brilliant rally to cut our 22-point lead to two, and this had not happened in any previous game. I watched them as we dressed for a late Sunday afternoon workout. They just didn't look good. How could we loosen them up?

Although our practice was not planned to be formal, as we took the floor I even cast aside what schedule I had. Near the close, still not liking the way they were reacting, I made up my mind to do something I never thought I'd do: I decided we'd finish practice with a "dunk shot" drill. No team of mine had done that since they outlawed the shot after Alcindor's sophomore season. When I told them to dunk, the change was almost miraculous. That little bit of levity dissipated all the tension. They were alive. They moved more quickly, with better speed and greater determination.

That dunking drill seemed to do more to ready us for Memphis State, both mentally and emotionally, than any other immediate preparation. If you ask me why, I can't tell you. All I can say is that it gave us the lift we needed to relax.

Very probably the drill may have relaxed Bill more than anyone else, because he dearly loves to dunk the basketball. His performance in that game was one of the finest by an individual that I have ever seen, not only from my own particular team and players, but from any player I've seen in any championship series. Only in the 1965 finals when Gail Goodrich scored 42 points—the record Bill broke—can you find a comparable effort.

In view of Gail's height (only 6′ 1″) his play was truly amazing. But regardless of Bill's advantage in that respect (he is 6′ 11″), his play was equally amazing. He showed tremendous timing and body balance as he handled those lob passes and hit twenty-one out of twenty-two shots from the floor. And he could have had twenty-four out of twenty-five, because he had three taken away for offensive goal interference.

The basketball world lauded Walton for that effort and rightly so. Bill, however, will quickly tell you that it was Lee's fourteen and Hollyfield's nine assists that enabled him to have such a stunning night.

It's ironic that Bill played that well. Some of the media during our four days in St. Louis had Bill jumping the team and about to sign with the pros. The rumor ballooned so out of proportion that the true story never did appear.

When we arrived in St. Louis there were no seven-foot beds at our hotel. After sleeping Friday night in a regular bed, Bill acknowledged that the semifinal win over Indiana had completely exhausted him. J. D. Morgan, our athletic director, who had a second room at another hotel, the Chase Park Plaza, informed us that it had a king-size bed, and, while we don't like to divide our players, we decided to transfer Bill to his room. But about 1:00 A.M. on Sunday, however, Bill was ejected from the room because the room clerk had mistakenly sold it. That left Bill in the lobby without any room in which to sleep. Finally, after determined efforts by Mr. Morgan, Gary Cunningham, and a sportswriter, we got Bill back in a room with a king-size bed. And, as we always do with our players to insure more privacy, we cut off calls to his room.

The next morning, writers tried to find Bill at the team's hotel and at the Chase Park Plaza, but of course they couldn't. So the story exploded that Bill had jumped the club, quit the team, and was in hiding waiting to sign a contract with a pro team. This was not the case at all. While Bill spent the rest of the nights at the Chase Park Plaza, he took all his meals with the team, as well as participating in all the practices and meetings.

Some writers tried to predict all kinds of dire things, and a lot of them got burned, so to speak, assuming something had happened without getting the facts. These are the things about the media that disturb Bill. Naturally a very reticent, quiet young man who doesn't want to be uncooperative, Bill is an entirely different person from what the press often implies. The claim that he dislikes to grant interviews probably arises from the fact that immediately after a game Bill wants to get away quickly and relax. He probably expends as much individual energy as any player I've ever coached. This, coupled with his aversion to large crowds, seems to create difficulties for him with the media. But as Bill matures, he has been giving them more time. After the NCAA, for instance, in Atlanta, Georgia, where he received the Naismith trophy (basketball's equivalent to the Heisman trophy in football), he was a very fine, cooperative, and willing interviewee, and the media seemed pleased with his honesty and openness.

Who is to say how Bill feels physically after a game? I doubt if I have ever had a player go through so much to play. He has to get to the arena a good hour before the rest of the team to use heat hydroculators on his knees, a treatment he keeps up until we go on the floor. After the game, he spends another thirty to forty-five minutes sitting with his knees packed in ice so they won't swell. Every day we practice or play, Bill has to go through this same routine. That alone nearly doubles the time he devotes to basketball in comparison to most other players.

This season Bill was given permission to call a timeout whenever he felt he needed one. This is a rare privilege, but no one I've ever coached has had a knee problem like Walton's. During our thirty games, there were times Bill elected to call time out when I would have preferred not to. But no one can see into those knees. Only Bill can judge when they are causing him such trouble that it's best to give them a rest.

Bill was also charged with having special privilege because he was allowed to judge whether or not he practiced the Monday following a game. Again, he is the first player I've given that option, but that was because of the nature of his physical problem. I am sure Bill would not want to skip practice.

Missing Mondays seemed to be beneficial to Bill. Indirectly his absence was quite beneficial to the team too, in that it allowed me to give more work and attention to Nater and Drollinger. They'd get a good go against each other, a welcome respite from having to work against Bill, who is so awesome on defense that I sometimes feared it might destroy their incentive. Each also had a good workout against a different style of play.

All our players are individuals. They may have a different outlook on life from the youth of five years ago and even more different from my age group at that point in time. Occasionally we all—coaches, media, spectators—expect too much from them. Sometimes we tend to see them as outstanding performers and forget how young they still are. We need only to analyze ourselves to realize that we adults do not always act like adults in everything we do.

These talented young men of the 1972–73 UCLA basketball team are part of a win streak of seventy-five straight games. Who can say where it will go? They and those before them have won forty-three games without defeat in our conference, the Pacific Eight; they have won thirty-five games in a row on the road; but, what I believe is the most impressive statistic of all—our teams have won thirty-six games without defeat in NCAA tournament play.

Yes, this was a remarkable group who fulfilled all that was expected of them and more. The season was a trying one for me, primarily because of my little heart flare-up, but the end result was extremely gratifying and made this one of the most cherished of all our championships.

28

*Talent is God-given, be humble;
Fame is man-given, be thankful:
Conceit is self-given, be careful.*

NO MATTER HOW you total success in the coaching profession it all comes down to a single factor—talent. There may be a hundred great coaches of whom you never have heard in basketball, football, or any sport who will probably never receive the acclaim they deserve simply because they have not been blessed with the talent. Although not every coach can win consistently with talent, no coach can win without it.

Over the years, particularly in the last decade or so, I have been fortunate. UCLA has had some remarkably talented basketball players. There is sufficient talent right here in Los Angeles that you need go no farther to search for it. Often I've heard that our success is due to the out-of-state boys who have come to Westwood. We have had some great ones, to be sure—like Alcindor, Hazzard, Warren, Lucius Allen, Bibby, to name a few. But we have also had some remarkable players from our own southern California area—players like Wicks, Rowe, Green, Cunningham, Patterson, Naulls, Erickson, Goodrich, Vallely, Lacey, Walton, Wilkes, and others.

Within ninety miles of our campus, there is a fountain of talent unequaled anywhere else in America except, perhaps, in other really large metropolitan areas. We don't get it all, but we get our share and that's all we ask. Probably 90 percent, or possibly more, of our time is spent evaluating youngsters right here, with the remainder elsewhere in California, the Northwest, and in other states.

We do not initiate contact with players from out of state; usually they contact us by some means—coach, principal, or mutual friend. Then we may look at a film or talk to people whom we respect about them. If the prospect meets our entrance requirements and fits in with our player needs, we may then extend a scholarship offer.

We have considerable competition for the talent in our immediate area. We have two strong basketball powers right at hand in USC and Cal State Long Beach, and of course everyone else in the Pac Eight, the state colleges, and the smaller colleges on the West Coast looks here also. And the rest of the nation has long since discovered that this is a large fountain of talent.

Although it is probably no different from other schools in our conference, we have a pretty good built-in scouting system of our own. We have a rather large, interested alumni group of former players and managers who have a good eye for basketball talent. Some are coaches now, others officials, but most are still buffs who love to watch the game whether it be on a local playground, a neighborhood high school, or junior college. Hardly a day goes by during basketball season that one of my former players doesn't call to tell me about a prospect he's seen. We even have a father or two—Marvin Lee, Greg's father, for instance—who has a son we can use.

There is one tremendous advantage to this. Each of those men (I have to pick that word carefully, because even though they may be fathers they are still youngsters to me) is well versed in the Wooden philosophy. They know what I want in a young man, and what it takes to play here. They automatically eliminate many, which is a fine screening system for us. Of course, I don't want to imply that my former players spend day and night seeking talent, but if they see someone they believe is a bona fide prospect, they call.

Among the most active alumni supporters of our program are the ex-managers. They were largely responsible for organizing an annual dinner meeting for the alumni group. Held in January at the recreation center on the UCLA campus, it has had an amazing turnout, particularly among those alumni from my earlier years. Many of the ex-managers haven't missed a game for years. No more loyal friends could be found anywhere than such men as Steve Aranoff, Gary Walls, Ted Henry, Dennis Minichian, George Morgan, Harold Crawford, Bill Anderson, Herb Furth, and numerous others who have served in that position. Quite a number of them still work with us charting shots, turnovers, and other statistics that aren't normally provided in every game. Some of them have never missed a home game, a few go on the road, and some have seen all of our NCAA championship games. Furthermore, it is a labor of love, on their own time and at their own expense.

The managers, over all these years, have been steadfastly devoted to our team. They are friends I value dearly, and young men of whom I am equally as proud as of the boys who played in the games. No honor is more fulfilling than the accomplishments of the young men you have worked with so closely—players or managers, All-American or average.

Honors are fleeting, just as fame is; I cherish friendship more. I am very flattered, very honored and very appreciative of the fact that in 1960 I was elected to the Basketball Hall of Fame as a player and in 1972 as a coach, the only man to date to be in the Hall in a dual capacity. While such an honor is great recognition for any man in his profession, I didn't get there alone. Every man who has been with me from my grammar school days on a dirt court in Centerton, or in Martinsville, Purdue, Dayton, South Bend, Indiana State, or UCLA holds a share of such honors. They have all been kind to me in helping me achieve what success has been mine. Their contribution reminds me of these few words from Lao-Tse:

> Kindness in words creates confidence,
> Kindness in thinking creates profoundness,
> Kindness in giving creates love.

I hope that in some way each of my boys, whether he may now be fifty or just eighteen, will understand somewhat why I do things the way I do. From my friends in the media, I keep getting one persistent question. "John," they ask, "when you retire, will you pick your all-time team?"

I give an immediate answer, always the same: "Never."

Can I truthfully say whether Lewis Alcindor is better than Bill Walton? Who are the two best of all the guards—Eddie Sheldrake, Dick Banton, Walt Hazzard, John Green, Mike Warren, Ron Livingston, Don Johnson, Morris Taft, Walt Torrence, George Stanich, Lucius Allen, Gail Goodrich, Henry Bibby, and others? Who are the two best of all the forwards—Alan Sawyer, Willie Naulls, John Moore, Jerry Norman, Dick Ridgway, Don Bragg, Gary Cunningham, Keith Erickson, Pete Blackman, Jack Hirsch, Curtis Rowe, Keith Wilkes, Sidney Wicks, and others?

Who can say which ones should rank above the others? My only reply is that at the given time in the given year the man doing the job was doing his best. For that moment, he was the best that played for me. I have always contended that the great players of a past era, if transported into the present with the fine coaching, the fine equipment and the fine facilities now available, would be every bit as great as those men being called superstars today.

Players who have attained that pinnacle in my regime as a coach have done so on individual merit, but in all honesty I feel that their accomplishment is at least partially indebted to having come within our system. Nevertheless, though the system has given many an opportunity, it couldn't make the man unless the latent talent were present.

An immediate example is Keith Erickson. He blossomed into greatness by hard, diligent work, but his ultimate success depended upon those who surrounded him and worked just as diligently as he to make the system an effective, dynamic force. Of course, he had to possess the inherent ability and competitive spirit.

Another striking example of ultimate individual success through melding into our system was Sidney Wicks. On and off the bench as a sophomore, Sidney acquired a partial understanding of the system as a junior, truly found it in the USC game and the NCAA championship against Jacksonville that year, and became totally accomplished within its limits as a senior.

In his final year of 1970–71, Sidney became the dominant force. It was one of the few times in my career that a forward had done so. He directed us at both ends of the floor and when the pressure became the greatest, the players went to him. Innately possessed of great individual talent, Sidney subordinated his personal desires to fill the need of the team. A genuinely great performer has such supreme confidence in his own ability that he is not afraid to take that risk.

Sidney genuinely personified what an individual can accomplish within the bounds and limitation of our system. He has reached as close to the maximum potential as a young man can. Most of it came together when he was able to channel his emotional and physical abilities into our team effort. If Sidney is able to sustain this meld, he could be as fine an all-around forward as professional basketball has ever seen. His physical attributes are truly amazing.

Those who saw Sidney's last performance for UCLA in the Astrodome in Houston in the NCAA finals remember his brilliance. It's an example I continue to point out to equally talented youngsters as they come along. When Villanova was pressing us hard, Sidney was the man we had bring the ball down court, in spite of the fact that he was playing on a very sore foot. He was an excellent dribbler and ball handler, and I knew that no one would outmuscle such a courageous competitor in a pressure situation.

That was an inspiring night. What a contrast it was to the earlier game with Houston that year when Alcindor was hurt. This time, with the game all but over, there was no way we could lose our seventh NCAA. As the ball came down toward our end of the floor for Henry Bibby to shoot two free throws, there were just seconds to go.

The benches in the Astrodome are below floor level, and all of a sudden Sidney came over to the pit. Forgotten was the little difficulty that we had had only a day or two before. Sidney, exuberantly happy as he leaned over and grabbed my hand, literally radiated his feelings. A smile covered his whole face and his eyes were sparkling.

"Coach," he said, "it's been great. A great career, coach."

With that he bounded back onto the floor. As I waved my program and yelled my thanks for a fantastic effort, he suddenly stopped, turned back, and declared:

"Coach, you're really something."

Yes, as Glennice Harmon has put it so eloquently in her poem "They Ask Me Why I Teach," where else could I find such splendid company?

ACKNOWLEDGMENTS

My THANKS to my wife, who read and reread every word in every stage of production, and to Jack Tobin, who worked closely with me in constructing our hours of interview into this narrative.

I am also deeply grateful to J. D. Morgan, UCLA's athletic director; my secretary, Mrs. Jean Dunne; UCLA's photographers, Stan Troutman and Norm Schindler; UCLA's sports information director, Vic Kelley, and his assistant, Frank Stewart; to Mrs. Peggy Fauquier and Mrs. Betty Martin, who transcribed our interview tapes; to Mrs. Peggy Veselka, who typed the finished manuscript; and especially to our editors, Floyd Thatcher, vice president and executive editor of Word Books, and Mrs. Pat Wienandt of the editorial staff, who shepherded the project through every step.

ABOUT JACK TOBIN

In his forty-plus years as journalist, Jack Tobin has covered every facet of news from homicides to presidential elections, Super Bowls to sandlot football games, tree plantings to a two-year investigation of James R. Hoffa and the Teamsters' Union pension fund. He has freelanced for such magazines as *Time, Life, Look, Saturday Evening Post, Fortune,* and *Sports Illustrated*. Since 1962, he has been *Sports Illustrated* correspondent for Southern California, handling story suggestions and assignment of photographers, artists, and writers—one of the largest geographic responsibilities in the magazine's system of correspondents.

Jack's love for writing dates from a December Saturday in 1930, when at age ten he first saw the Los Angeles Memorial Coliseum, a Notre Dame football team, and a legend of the era named Knute Rockne. That night, flat on the floor of his Long Beach home, Jack tried to join such famed Los Angeles sportswriters as the late Mark Kelly and the late Bill Henry in reporting on Notre Dame's stunning 27–0 upset of USC.

That desire soon reached reality for Jack. Ever since joining the *Long Beach Press-Telegram* as a teenager, he has used words as a way of life and livelihood, except for three years active duty on a Navy attack transport during World War II. From the *Press-Telegram,* he became part of the original staff of the *Los Angeles Mirror* (later the *Mirror-News*) in 1948, and in 1961 joined the *Los Angeles Times*.

Tobin has also held a number of executive positions. In 1962 he began a four and a half year stint as director of public relations, promotions, and advertising for the Memorial Coliseum Commission in Los Angeles, where he handled two of the largest spectator facilities in the nation, the Memorial Coliseum and the Memorial Sports Arena. In 1966, he was appointed executive vice president of the Los Angeles Toros in the newly born National Professional Soccer League. Following the sale and transfer of that franchise, he became vice president and director of marketing for Computicket Corporation, a computerized ticket and reservation system.

Tobin holds two degrees in journalism, the B.A. from Notre Dame University (1943) and the M.S. from UCLA (1959). He and his wife, Virginia, and their son, Timothy, who is a graduate student in theater arts at UCLA, reside in Playa del Rey, California.

We Deliver!
And So Do These Bestsellers.

- [ ] THE PETER PRINCIPLE by Peter & Hull (5433—$1.25)
- [ ] EVERYTHING YOU ALWAYS WANTED TO KNOW ABOUT SEX by Dr. David Rubin (5570—$1.95)
- [ ] CHARIOTS OF THE GODS? by Erich Von Daniken (5753—$1.25)
- [ ] I KNOW WHY THE CAGED BIRD SINGS by Maya Angelou (5848—$1.25)
- [ ] I'VE GOT TO TALK TO SOMEBODY, GOD by Marjorie Holmes (6566—$1.25)
- [ ] FUTURE SHOCK by Alvin Toffler (6700—$1.95)
- [ ] LINDA GOODMAN'S SUN SIGNS (6719—$1.50)
- [ ] THE GREENING OF AMERICA by Charles Reich (6767—$1.95)
- [ ] BURY MY HEART AT WOUNDED KNEE by Dee Brown (7077—$1.95)
- [ ] GUINNESS BOOK OF WORLD RECORDS by The McWhirters (7152—$1.50)
- [ ] GODS FROM OUTER SPACE by Erich Von Daniken (7276—$1.25)
- [ ] BOBBY FISCHER TEACHES CHESS (7397—$1.95)
- [ ] WUNNERFUL, WUNNERFUL by Lawrence Welk (7466—$1.75)
- [ ] GAME OF THE FOXES by Ladislas Farago (7477—$1.95)
- [ ] THE CALL TO GLORY by Jeane Dixon (7512—$1.25)
- [ ] BEYOND FREEDOM AND DIGNITY by B. F. Skinner (7549—$1.95)

Buy them at your local bookstore or use this handy coupon for ordering:

Bantam Books, Inc., Dept. NFB, 414 East Golf Road, Des Plaines, Ill. 60016

Please send me the books I have checked above. I am enclosing $_____ (please add 25¢ to cover postage and handling). Send check or money order—no cash or C.O.D.'s please.

Mr/Mrs/Miss_____

Address_____

City_____State/Zip_____

NFB—7/73

Please allow three weeks for delivery. This offer expires 7/74.

FREE!
Bantam Book Catalog

It lists over a thousand money-saving bestsellers originally priced from $3.75 to $15.00—bestsellers that are yours now for as little as 50¢ to $2.25!

The catalog gives you a great opportunity to build your own private library at huge savings!

So don't delay any longer—send for your catalog TODAY! It's absolutely FREE!

Just send us a post card with the
information below or use this handy coupon:

BANTAM BOOKS, INC.
Dept. FC, 414 East Golf Road, Des Plaines, Ill. 60016

Mr./Mrs./Miss_____
(please print)
Address_____
City_____State_____Zip_____

Do you know someone who enjoys books? Just give us their names and addresses and we'll send them a FREE CATALOG too!

Mr./Mrs./Miss_____
Address_____
City_____State_____Zip_____

Mr./Mrs./Miss_____
Address_____
City_____State_____Zip_____

FC—3/73